Anonymous

History of the Work of the Board of Trade of Portland, Maine

Anonymous

History of the Work of the Board of Trade of Portland, Maine

ISBN/EAN: 9783744692922

Printed in Europe, USA, Canada, Australia, Japan

Cover: Foto ©ninafisch / pixelio.de

More available books at **www.hansebooks.com**

HISTORY

OF THE WORK

OF THE

BOARD OF TRADE

OF PORTLAND, MAINE.

What it has Originated and Accomplished Since its Organization;
Constitution and By-Laws, Original and Present Membership.

WITH ILLUSTRATIONS.

Compiled and Published under direction of the Board,
by the Secretary.
1887.

PREFACE.

To answer an oft repeated inquiry as to the object of the Board of Trade, and what it has done for the benefit of Portland, as well as to preserve its past history for the guidance and satisfaction of those who may administer its affairs in future, and in accordance with a vote of the Board of Managers, adopted May 6, 1886, I have endeavored to briefly sketch a digest of its most important work, or so much as would be of interest to perpetuate in history, together with such reference to the men identified more prominently with that work, as these limits permit.

The Records of the Board having been destroyed in the great fire of '66, I have been obliged to draw chiefly upon memory for whatever did not appear in public print during the first ten years of the Board's existence. But I am satisfied that with my five annual reports of the Trade and Commerce of Portland, published by the Board previous to 1874, and the following sketches, that a fairly intelligent nucleus is furnished for the future historian of the Board.

M. N. RICH, *Secretary.*

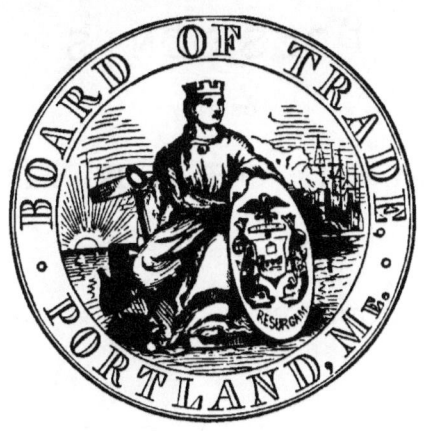

THE OFFICIAL SEAL

Representing the Goddess of Commerce seated in the foreground with the left arm reclining on the corporate seal of the city of Portland, while the right hand clutches the anchor of Hope, and the rising sun illuminates the shipping and other emblems of Commerce in the back or water prospective, the whole being encircled with the official title of the corporation. The seal was designed by Secretary Rich and adopted by the Board in 1864.

PRESIDENTS

OF THE

BOARD OF TRADE.

WILLIAM W. WOODBURY,	1853.*
JOHN B. BROWN,	1853 to 1863.
T. C. HERSEY,	{ 1863 to 1868. { 1873 to 1874.
JONAS H. PERLEY,	1868 to 1870.
WOODBURY S. DANA,	1870 to 1873.
GEORGE W. WOODMAN,	1874 to 1878.
CHARLES H. HASKELL,	1878 to 1879.
SAMUEL J. ANDERSON,	1879 to 1883.
GEORGE P. WESCOTT,	1883 to 1885.
JOSEPH E. BLABON,	1885 to

* Resigned.

William W. Woodbury.

Mr. Woodbury was elected as the first President of the Board on account of his public spirit and the hearty support that he gave towards effecting its organization, but press of business did not justify his acceptance, and he shortly after resigned the office. Subsequently he took an active part in the formation of the Merchants Exchange, of which he was a charter member.

John B. Brown.

Mr. Brown was the first active President of the Board, and filled the office for ten successive years, the longest term held by any other presiding officer. His administration was characterized with a vigor that at once insured the prosperity of the Board, and demonstrated its usefulness in aiding the developments and shaping the progress of the city, at the new business era upon which it was then just entering. Mr Brown's interest in the Board never flagged, and his opinions and advice on business matters was always regarded as sound, and his council on public affairs always had great weight; he was a recognized leader among his fellowmen.

Theophilus C. Hersey.

Mr. Hersey probably devoted more time and care, and held the interests of the Board of Trade nearer to his heart than any other man of his day. From its organization to the day of his death, in 1886, he ever evinced a warm interest and for most of the time, and at his death, was one of its Board of Managers. He served two terms as President, and was forced to decline further honors in the chair on account of failing health. He was also for several years Vice President of the National Board of Trade, and reflected honor and credit upon the constituent organization that he for so many years represented with such entire acceptance to the National Board The constant press of business in which he was so industriously involved, never

JOHN B. BROWN.

prevented him from attending all its meetings with marked regularity and promptness, and it is doing no injustice to others to say that he was one of the most devoted and useful members that the Board has ever had, and that he has left a record that few, if any, will equal in the future history of the Board.

JONAS H. PERLEY.

Mr. Perley was a very acceptable and dignified presiding officer, and the older members of the Board remember his pleasant companionship and conscientious efforts in all his duties to the Board. An active. prosperous business man at the time, he took deep interest in the establishment of water communication with the eastern ports of the State and was for a time agent of the Eastern Packet Co., until he removed to the West, where he has experienced rather a varied fortune, but his many friends here remember him for his unselfish public spirit and devotion to the common prosperity of his former home in years agone.

WOODBURY S. DANA.

Mr. Dana was one of the most prompt and business-like presiding officers that the Board has ever had; always in the chair at the appointed hour, the gavel would fall whether a quorum was present or not. The members soon caught this spirit of promptness, and business was jogged off with less delay and more satisfaction to business men. Pleasant and affable in the chair, alive to all the duties of the hour, Mr. Dana's is remembered as one of the most useful and pleasant administrations in the work of the Board. Mr. Dana has been long in the Board of Management and is closely identified with all its work, in which he takes a lively interest to this day.

GEORGE W. WOODMAN.

Mr. Woodman, from the organization of the Board through all its years of service down to the present time, has been always faithful and constant in all his varied duties to the organization, probably no one making greater sacrifices than Mr. Woodman to promote the welfare of the Board and its work, with a force and zeal that has always commanded the highest respect and deferance of his associates. As presiding officer he possessed the good qualification of dignity, promptness and clearness of decision, and a familiarity with parliamentary usages that was of great advantage to him in discussions and the ready dispatch of business. He is regarded as one of the bulwarks of the Board and is held in the highest respect by all its members.

CHARLES H. HASKELL.

Mr. Haskell was a sharp and vivacious man, and his quick and ready conception and honest fidelity to his convictions, made him an enthusiast in whatever business he engaged, hence he was ever characterized as a power in whatever station he filled, and his long and faithful services on the Board of Management, as Treasurer for nine years, well equipped him for the position of presiding officer, which he discharged with much ability and acceptance.

SAMUEL J. ANDERSON.

General Anderson was a vigorous and dignified presiding officer. Courteous to his associates, he discharged the duties of his office with a dash and firmness that carried the honest convictions of his fidelity to the duties of his office, and on public occasions was a brilliant exponent of the business interests of his city and State, always possessing a keene appreciation of the responsibilities of his office, and exercised great care to subordinate his own private opinions to the will of the majority, and is still in the Board of Management, and much respected.

GEORGE P. WESCOTT.

Mr. Wescott was one of the most industrious and pleasant officers that has filled the chair. Of large business experience, he grappled with the most intricate questions with an irresistable force and persistance that made his administration one of continued success, and the Board did not flag in interest nor power while he was at its head, and he vacated the office much to the regret of his associates, and carried in his retirement the universal good wishes of all.

Joseph E. Blabon.

Mr. Blabon, now filling the chair of President for the second term, is a very popular and able officer, and though naturally of quiet and unpretentious disposition, commands the universal respect of his fellow citizens and of all the members of the Board. He patiently and persistently studies the duties of the Board in all matters of public interest, and vigorously pursues and pushes the influence of the Board to accomplish, ultimately, the work of his convictions. His administration promises to be one of the most prosperous and successful in its already long line of faithful servants.

Treasurers.

Mr. Jonas H. Perley was elected treasurer at the organization in 1853, and appears to have served until 1860, and was succeeded by Orlando M. Marrett, who served from 1860 to 1864. Then Charles H. Haskell from 1864 to 1874, when Augustus E. Stevens was elected treasurer, but shortly after resigned, and Charles S. Fobes was elected in 1874, and has been successively re-elected every year since, and in that capacity has been a very valuable member of the Board of Management in debates and as a counselor.

Secretaries.

Henry Fox, Esq., was the first secretary of the Board, being elected at the organization in 1853, and was succeeded by John Q. Twitchell in 1862, who served till 1864. Marshall N. Rich succeeded Mr. Twitchell in January, 1864, and has been unanimously re-elected every succeeding year; and since the death of Mr. Porter, of Baltimore, last year, is now the oldest Secretary in continued service in the United States.

Who have been Active Members.

Without intending any invidious distinction, but rather to bear in pleasant recollection their devoted and earnest efforts in behalf of the public interests that involved the attention of the Board from time to time, in the past twenty-five years, and whose names do not otherwise appear in official prominence, we recall the names of the following members, who in their day have either held offices or have been identified with the active workers in the Board, viz: Capt. John B Coyle, Fred'k Davis, John A. Poor, John M. Wood, Thos. R. Jones, John Purrington, Rufus E. Wood, N. J. Miller, John G. Tolford, N. P. Woodbury, Wm. H. Foye, John True, Wm. Chase, Cyrus S. Clark, Capt. Chas. M. Davis, Capt. Wm. Ross, Capt. E. D. Choate, Capt. S. Blanchard, Capt. Dan'l Hood, Samuel Tyler, T. C. Stevens, James Olcott Brown, Orlando M. Marrett, Luther Dana, James S. Bedlow, Ira J. Batchelder, Thos. R. Hayes, James Freeman, A. K. Shurtleff, Wm. L. Southard, Jos. Hale, J. W. Dyer, Benj. Stevens Jr, Jas. E. Fernald, Thos. E. Twitchell, Warren Brown, Alvah Conant, Edwin Churchill, Rensalaer Cram, Andrew Spring, A. L. Hobson, Isaac Jackson, Hosea Kendall, Frank O. Libby, Abner Lowell, John Randall, Joseph Wescott, H. I. Robinson, Augustus E. Stevens, Wm. A. Winship, Samuel E. Spring, Israel Washburn, Jr., Edmund Phinney, A. H. F. Furbush, Chas. McLaughlin.

And of those still living, but who have retired from the more active duties of business, and do not so often appear in the councils of the Board, we might in this connection recognize the former good work of the following, we trust without exciting the jealousy of the younger recognized active members:— Oliver Gerrish, Ezra Carter, John C. Proctor, E. E. Upham, Moses Gould, Reuben Kent, Thos. H. Weston, Geo. F. Foster, Chas. A. Stackpole, Edward M. Patten, Wm. Deering, Chas. P. Kimball, J. W. Waterhouse, J. W. Munger, Jacob McLellan, Jas. L. Farmer, Washington Ryan, Daniel F. Emery.

T. C. HERSEY.

THE BOARD OF TRADE:

Its Origin, and History of its Progress.

At the commencement of the new era in the modes and methods of business, that so generally pervaded the length and breadth of this country more than a quarter of a century ago, by the introduction of rapid transit and swift communication; when the attention of the world was being directed to the geographical advantages of terminal points, and Portland was beginning to realize the dawn of European commerce by direct steamship lines—the fruition of its hopes—centered in the unrivaled advantages of location, climate, depth of water, shore line, proximity to so much and valuable water power—its most sagacious people could foresee that, in the great race of competition for power and greatness, even her share of the commerce of the world was not to be dropped in the lap of Portland without steady and persistant effort and struggle even to keep pace in the "jostle and scramble" then already so apparent, that leading business men became firmly impressed that the greatest efficiency could only be realized through the united efforts of the various interests and industries of the city and State, in an organization representing these interests in such manner as to voice the wishes and will of the people in the most effective manner. Accordingly the project of a BOARD OF TRADE was considered, and a meeting called for *organization* at the rooms of the Mercantile Library Association, in Free St., on the ninth of May, 1853.

The fundamental principals of such organization were ably set forth by its projectors, and embodied the following general ideas: "That the efforts of the Board be directed to give tone and energy to the various branches of trade, and in securing the advantages which the position of the city offers to commerce and manufactures, consider all subjects of internal improvements agitated in the community, brought before the Board by its members; and where legislation is required in making such improvements, direct its efforts in a firm and vigorous manner to encourage and promote in every possible way its commercial and industrial progress, so as to give the fullest development to all the natural advantages of the port, and provide for speedy and ample transportation of merchandise throughout the State; adjust matters relating to trade, and to establish such customs and ordinances as shall secure and maintain a unity of action for the public good; and such general supervision of the harbor necessary to prevent encroachments and secure sufficient depth of water; establish port regulations and suitable harbor and coast defences so as to render it safe at all times, and to facilitate in every possible way encouragement of commerce, and to prevent discrimination to our disadvantage in the movement of merchandise on the sea, or on the land:" the importance also of bringing the merchants and business men together once a day on 'change from 12½ until 1 o'clock P. M., in front of the Post Office, in order to cultivate and promote a business acquaintance and to unite in mutual efforts to enhance the interests of all, was recognized as an element to be promoted by the organization.

After discussing whether to adopt the name of "Chamber of Commerce" or "Board of Trade" the latter title was adopted, together with the following:

Preamble—Believing in the necessity of an association of citizens to give tone and energy to their efforts in securing the advantages which the position of the city offers to commerce, trade and manufactures; as well as to promote unity of action, and to cultivate a more intimate and friendly acquaintance among the business men of the city; and that these ends may be obtained by the establishment of a Board of Trade: We, citizens of Portland, do therefore agree to form such an association, and to be governed by the constitution and code of by-laws

The organization was completed by the choice of the following officers:

PRESIDENT,
*WM. W. WOODBURY.

VICE PRESIDENTS,
*JEDEDIAH JEWETT,   H. J. LIBBY.   *T. C. HERSEY,

DIRECTORS,
JAMES L. FARMER,   *CHAS. M. DAVIS,
*EBEN STEELE,   *HIRAM COVELL,
GEO. W. WOODMAN,   *A. K. SHURTLEFF,
*JOHN C. BROOKS.

TREASURER,
JONAS H. PERLEY.

SECRERARY,
HENRY FOX.

COMMITTEE OF ARBITRATION,
*N. F. DEERING,   *A. L. HOBSON,
H. J. LIBBY,   *C. S. CARTER,
*CHARLES M. DAVIS.

PORT WARDENS,
*WM. CAMMETT,   *CHAS. M. DAVIS.

MEMBERS,

P. H. Brown,	J. H. Fletcher,	*J. W. Russell,
*Nath'l Blanchard,	J. B. Fillebrown,	*Jas. E. Robinson,
*Henry Bailey,	*Eliphalet Greely,	*Nath'l Ross,
*J. L. Boothby,	*Wm. Hammond,	*Abner Shaw,
*Alvah Conant,	*J. F. Hall,	*A. E. Stevens,
C. H. Cram,	*Edw. Howe,	Thos. Shaw,
N. O. Cram,	*Chas. H. Haskell,	*St. John Smith,
*Merritt Coolidge,	*Joseph Hale,	O. P. Shepherd,
Eben Corey.	H. H. Hay,	William Senter,
*Caleb S. Carter,	*A. L. Hobson,	*William Stewart,
John Conley,	*Robert Ilsley,	H. P. Storer,
*Charles E. Cram,	*Luther Jewett,	*Sam'l Tyler,
*Daniel L. Choate,	*William Kimball,	C. C. Tolman,
*Luther Dana,	*E. M. Leavitt,	*W. W. Woodbury,
W. S. Dana,	James W. Leavitt,	*John M. Wood,
*Fred'k Davis,	John Lynch,	*Rufus E. Wood,
*N. F. Deering,	James S. Marrett,	*Wm. H. Wood,
*Hophni Eaton,	*A. R. Mitchell,	Alfred Woodman,
*Daniel Evans,	*Reuben Ordway,	*S. B. Waite,
J. S. Fillebrown,	*Seward W. Porter,	Thomas H. Weston.
*Jas. E. Fernald,	*John Purington,	
*D. H. Furbish,	*J. C. Remick,	

* Deceased—54. Now living—25.

At a subsequent meeting Mr. Woodbury sent in his resignation as President, and John B. Brown, Esq., was unanimously elected to that office, to which he was afterwards successively re-elected until 1863, when he declined a further election, and was succeeded by Hon. T. C. Hersey.

INCORPORATION.

Early in the following year the Board of Trade, of Portland, was incorporated by the following Act of Legislature, approved March 22, 1854.

STATE OF MAINE.

In the year of our Lord one thousand eight hundred and fifty-four, an act to incorporate the Board of Trade, of Portland. Be it enacted by the Senate and House of Representatives in Legislature assembled, as follows:

SECTION 1. The Board of Trade of Portland, a voluntary association now existing in the city of Portland for the purpose of securing the advantages which the position of the city offers to commerce, trade and manufactures, is hereby created a body politic and corporate by the same name and with power to take by purchase, bequest, or otherwise, and to hold, transfer and convey real and personal property to the amount of fifty thousand dollars, the legal title of which shall be in the Board of Managers.

SECTION 2. Such corporation shall have power to prosecute and defend suits of law and in equity; to have and to use a common seal; to appoint two or more port wardens, and such number of pilots for the harbor of Portland, as said Board may deem necessary for the safety and convenience of the commerce of said port, and also to fix such compensation for the services of said pilots, as said Board may deem just and reasonable; also to appoint a committee of arbitration to decide all disputed accounts, contracts and controversies of a mercantile or commercial character that may be brought before said Committee by the members of said Board; and the present constitution and by-laws of said Board of Trade, not repugnant to the constitution and laws of this State, shall continue in force under said corporation until changed by the corporation; and shall have all the powers and privileges, and be subject to all the duties and liabilities belonging to similar corporations in this State.

IN THE HOUSE OF REPRESENTATIVES,
March 17th, 1854.

This bill having had three several readings, passed to be enacted.

FR'S G. BUTLER, *Speaker, pro tem.*

IN SENATE, March 18, 1854.

This bill having had two several readings, passed to be enacted.

S. STARK, *President, pro tem.*

March 22, 1854, Approved.

WM. G. CROSBY.

The existing constitution and by-laws were subsequently adopted and are in force to-day.

THE EARLY HISTORY OF THE BOARD

Was not unlike that of kindred organizations of its day, of other and larger municipalities, attracting but little attention nor carrying much influence until it began to operate in the developement of commerce, and in extending manufacturing interests and shaping the City's natural advantages with a power and influence not hitherto reached, giving a vigorous co-operation soon felt and recognised abroad as an agency destined to place Portland in her proper rank among the commercial cities of the world.

Before the Board had a permanent home, its meetings were held for a while in the Mercantile Library Rooms in the Free Street Block, in the "Fox Block," on Middle Street, and occasionally at Mr. Brown's counting room, or at Collector Jewett's office in the Custom House, until it moved to its present locality on Exchange Street, in 1863.

The greatest and most important event in the first year's history of the Board was the Dinner given at Lancaster Hall, on the twentieth of December, 1853, in honor of the arrival of the British Steamer, Sarah Sands at this port, this being the pioneer ship in the opening of regular steam communication between Europe and Portland. The event was a momentous one for Portland, and was creditably recognized and commemorated by her citizens, in which the Board of Trade figured most conspicuously.

The Sarah Sands, a steamship of 1300 tons, belonging to the Canadian Steam Navigation Company, commanded by Captain Washington Ilsley, a native of Portland, left Liverpool for Portland on the 28th of November, 1853, with two hundred and five passengers and full freight, making the passage in eighteen days and ten hours—her arrival was heralded by the ringing of bells and the firing of cannon—the whole town soon filled the streets and covered the wharves, and great was the pomp and circumstance surrounding the occasion. The Board of Trade having previously invited the notables and dignataries of Canada connected with the Steamship Company, as well as with the Atlantic and St. Lawrence Railroad Company, to be present at a Banquet to be given here three days after the arrival of the Sarah Sands, consequently there was quite a large "foreign element" present to welcome the event. Probably if the whole of England should be dumped into Portland harbor to-day it would not create more consternation and "fuss" than did the "Sarah Sands" swinging at her anchor in our harbor on that day of her arrival.

The two hundred and five passengers were fairly landed on the first day, also the mails, but it took about two weeks to unload and dispatch the cargo of a thirteen hundred ton ship, whereas now we see a six thousand ton ship discharged at our wharves in thirty-six hours; but Mr. Bellhouse the agent of the Sarah Sands insisted upon having all matters "amicably adjusted" before he would allow the unloading of the ship to proceed, and then no faster than the goods could be landed in good order.

On the next Monday, December twentieth, the Board of Trade celebrated the coming in of the Sarah Sands by a grand

JONAS H. PERLEY.

dinner at Lancaster Hall, on the corner of Congress and Centre Streets, erected by the late Hon. John B. Brown, who was then President of the Board of Trade, and who presided at the dinner. The occasion was made memorable by many happy incidents, and its success was largely due to Messrs. Jedediah Jewett, T. C. Hersey, Charles M. Davis, H. J. Libby, Edwin Churchill and George W. Woodman, who with the president constituted the committee.

The hall on this occasion was handsomely decorated, and the Lion and Eagle, surrounded by the national colors of both countries, were conspicuous among the decorations. The tables were elegantly spread, and the feast was prepared by Mr. R. L. Robinson; the bills of fare were printed on white satin. About six o'clock the company entered the hall, and the festivities were prolonged until a late hour in the evening.

The post-prandial exercises were opened by Mr. Jedediah Jewett, who gave us a toast "United States and Canada." This was followed by the band playing, "Hail, Columbia!" and "Rule, Britannia!" Rev. Dr. Carruthers, of the Second Parish, who had resided five years in Montreal, responded for Canada. He was followed in a short speech by Mr. Bellhouse, agent of the Canadian Navigation Company, which corporation, acting with the Atlantic & St. Lawrence Railroad, had chartered the first foreign steamer to this port. Mr. Bellhouse announced that the Sarah Sands was to be followed by the steamer "Cleopatra" (1500 tons) which would be the next ship dispatched to Portland.

Mayor J. B. Cahoon, in responding to the sentiment "The City of Portland," made the speech of welcome. It was a splendid effort.

The health of Capt. Ilsley was proposed, and as he rose to thank the assembly for the honor done him, the sweet strains of "Home, Sweet Home," were played by the band. The Captain spoke briefly, but to the point. His former associations with Portland were feelingly remembered, and while he congratulated our citizens upon the commercial outlook, he felt proud of the honor given him of bringing into port the first steamship of the line.

A toast was next given Judge William P. Preble, the first president of the Atlantic and St. Lawrence Railroad. Judge Preble was ill at home, but a note from him was listened to with pleasure. Hon. Josiah S. Little responded for the Grand Trunk Railway, remarks were made by Rev. Dr. Nichols, and Gen. Samuel Fessenden delivered a long and able speech.

The health of "Her Majesty the Queen," was proposed by Charles P. Ilsley, and in his allusions to the Sarah Sands the genial "Pic" was at his best. Mr. D. Starr, the British consul at this port, replied to the toast to Queen Victoria. Mr. Charles Holden, then editor of the Argus, responded for "the press of Portland and Montreal." Sir Alexander T. Galt, and many other Canadian notables, expected to attend the dinner, but could not reach this city in season.

Among other speakers of the evening are recalled the names of John A. Poor, Mr. Rynas of Montreal, Mr. Barnes, T. C. Hersey, Mr. Mitchell of Montreal, P. F. Varnum, C. A. Alexander, Capt. Edwin Churchill, J. B. Fillebrown, Henry Fox, Mr. Weston, Thomas H. Talbot, D. H. Furbush, and Mr. Duane. During the evening Mr. John Roberts favored the company with a fine song; and after several hours of enjoyment, the singing of "Auld Lang Syne" brought the festivities to a close, and thus the first complimentary dinner given by the Board of Trade passed into history as an occasion worthy of long rememberance.

The next dinner given by the Board was in 1856, to Capt. Wm. McMasters, of steamer Anglo-Saxon, the first ship of the Edmonstone, Allan & Co. line (which succeeded the Canadian line) and was served by Nathan J. Davis at the Commercial House, then situated on Fore street, opposite the present Custom House.

STEAMSHIP "GREAT EASTERN."

Next to the advent of the first steamer to Portland in importance that the Board of Trade had to grapple with in its early days, was the prospective coming to the "natural seaport" of the largest vessel in the world. Early in 1856 it was intimated that the "Great Eastern," then building in England, would probably make her first voyage to Portland on account of our abundant depth of water and safe anchorage for a ship of her great size (18,915 tons). The Board took the earliest opportunity to make ample arrangements to accommodate the great influx of visitors that the event promised to draw to the city and to provide suitable dockage, and co-operated with the city in the construction of the two large piers built for the purpose at a cost of $60,000, that stand to-day a monument of the public enterprise of the citizens of Portland of that day, though the ship never came; it was from no want of ample preparations on their part.

Coast Communication.

Previous to 1860 it had become evident to members of the Board, that not only the long line of sea coast towns but the British Maritime Provinces should be supplied with better and more speedy communication with this port, to invite the trade that would naturally seek our markets, with better facilities for moving goods, which discussions lead to the inception of the International Steamship Company; and the substantial and beautiful line of steamers that now ply between Portland and the lower Provinces and eastern seaport towns of the State, not only took its origin and has had the fostering care of this Board, but a regular line of sailing Packets was established by the Board, soon after, to reach all principal ports along the coast as far east as Jonesport and Machias, which subsequently eventuated in the Steamers DeWitt Clinton, to Rockland and Camden, the Charles Houghton to Waldoboro, and finally the establishment of the Portland and Machias Steamship Company, which brought thousands of dollars' worth of business to Portland from many ports that had not previously traded a dollars' worth in this market.

The Visit of Western Merchants.

Not only did the Board direct its attention to secure the eastern trade, to which the city was legitimately entitled, but it had now become patent to its members that it only wanted a better acquaintance of the people of the Western cities with our people and our advantages and opportunities for business, to bring a large trade, to secure an interchange of consignments. To this end, in June 1863, Mr. T. C. Hersey offered the following: "*Resolved*, that an inviation be extended to the Boards of Trade of Detroit, Chicago, and Milwaukee, to visit Portland at such time in July or August as may be agreed on by them." It was subsquently agreed to extend same invitation to the Montreal and Quebec Boards. The invitations were accepted and ample preparations made for their reception and entertainment, and on the evening of August 13th the several delegations arrived in this city, numbering about one hundred and twenty-five from Chicago, forty from Detroit, fifty from Milwaukee, and those from Canada with ladies accompanying Western delegates, made about two hundred and fifty visitors, many of whom received the kind hospitality of private residences, as guests of family circles; others, guests of the Board of Trade at the hotels, where the most liberal and sumptuous provisions were made for their comfort and pleasant sojourn while here. The delegations were formerly received by the citizens the following morning at the City Hall, where 'change was held from 11 until 2 o'clock P. M., and the guests welcomed to the hospitalities of the city by the President of the Board of Trade and the Mayor, and the time occupied in speech, sentiment and social intercourse, and in the evening the Board gave a levee and supper in City Hall, at which the ladies were invited, and which proved a brilliant affair and afforded great pleasure to our guests.

HIGH 'CHANGE AT CITY HALL.

The programme invited all to meet at eleven o'clock Friday, A. M., at the new City Hall, on 'change, for introduction to members of the Exchange and of the Board of Trade, and for a general hand shaking with the citizens. The black boards were in position there, and telegraphic bulletins displayed from time to time as fast as received throughout the morning. Merchandise and many special products of our city and State were displayed there in profusion, and for a while we enjoyed all the

WOODBURY S. DANA.

gush and bustle of a Western Board, and it was wonderful how the occasion drew out and widened the ideas of our people and how many "sharp corners" were knocked off at the Island excursion the next day, will never be wholly known. Like a bunch of keys the committee kept the "Brass Band" in their pockets during the whole time, and had music on all and every change in the programme, or as Porteous said "music all the time." The Island feast was at "Little Quohog Island," under the following committee of arrangements: T. C. Hersey, Jedediah Jewett, W. S. Dana, Jonas H. Perley, Wm. F. Safford, Henry Fox, John Lynch, O. M. Marrett, Thos. E. Twitchell, A. K. Shurtleff, James O. Brown, Wm. L. Southard, James E. Carter, J. B. Fillebrown, F. O. Libby, F. C. Moody, Geo. W. Woodman, E. E. Upham, Rensallear Cram, Chas. E. Jose, A. W. H. Clapp, Daniel F. Emery, M. N. Rich, H. I. Robinson, John Q. Twitchell, Jacob McLellan, Wm. W. Thomas, Rufus E. Wood, St. John Smith, H. Warren Lancy, Nathan Cummings, Horatio Hill, J. C. Stevens, Ezra Carter, Jr., Augustus E. Stevens, Warren Brown.

The Clam Bake.

Saturday morning the members of the Board and of the Merchants Exchange took their Western friends on an excursion among the islands in the steamer "Forest City," visiting the fortifications, the party numbering about fifteen hundred and landing on Diamond Island enjoyed a New England Clam Bake, the bill of fare including sixty bushels clams, ten bushels potatoes, sixty dozen ears corn, two hundred and fifty lobsters, ten bushels oysters, twenty codfish, eighty dozen eggs, eighty quarts baked beans, one hundred gallons coffee, sixty gallons ice cream and a good supply of other "fixings" necessary to enhance the "feast of wit and the flow of soul." The whole thing was a grand success and repeatedly acknowledged as such by our Western friends. Chicago in its official resolutions declared "That there is no record of such an excursion, so many miles of rail traveled free, such generous hospitalities and unbounded welcome that marked an era in the connection of the East with the West, one and indivisible now and forever," and the Detroit Board resolved "That never in the history of the country was an **excursion** of such imposing numbers, extended journey and useful purposes, so well devised and liberally accomplished, and the Milwaukee Chamber of Commerce resolved "Never was there a more generous invitation extended by the commercial men of an Atlantic city to their commercial bretheren in the West, than that by the Board of Trade of Portland, and none can ever be more successfully and completely carried out in all its details of enjoyment. The Detroit Commercial Advertiser said: "There were no mistakes, no jars, and whether at the reception, the excursion, or levee, every arrangement was complete, every preparation ample and everywhere we received the same courteous treatment, the same hospitality."

These and similiar personal expressions from most all of our visitors as well as results that have followed are reassuring that the objects of the Board were fully realized, indeed the results of acquaintances thus made, can scarcely be measured. Large consignments of flour and grain were soon made to Agencies here.

FLOUR INSPECTION.

The impetus given to the grain and flour trade by the visit of so many Western business men to Portland, soon suggested the necessity of a Flour Inspection for Portland to protect the reputation of sales made in this market and the Board of Trade early in that year appointed an efficient committee which established a *standard* for the various brands adopted by the trade, and the standard samples were deposited in the Board of Trade room for reference, and the Board was empowered to nominate the Inspector who was to hold the office only at the option of the Board, and to which body the Inspector was held responsible for the faithful and efficient discharge of his duties. This system continued with satisfactory results until the great fire of 1866 when the standard samples were destroyed, since, which, there has been less attention given to efficient inspection, and the trade, at least know that "Board of Trade" brands now sold in this market are only nominally so.

Discriminating Rates of Freight.

Late in 1862 considerable complaint was made by our merchants that freight from the West, for Boston via Portland, over the Grand Trunk road, was taking the preference in regard to dispatch as well as rates of freight, and that at certain seasons during heavy movements, Portland's local freight was often refused, to give dispatch to through freight to Boston, even at less rates than was exacted for Portland, hence Portland merchants complained that such ruinous and unfair competition was working badly for Portland, and the Board took the earliest measures to have Manager Brydges meet the Board in conference, upon the subject, which he did and denied the whole complaint, or a knowledge of any such injustice, and promised if there was any grounds for complaint to have such obsticles removed. But the trouble was not entirely cured, till the citizens took a determined and effective action, for a competing through line to the West, of which we speak more fully later on.

Steam Cruisers.

In the early part of the Rebellion, after the Revenue Cutter, Caleb Cushing had been destroyed by the "Tacony Pirates," and the exposed and unprotected condition of our harbor and towns along the extended line of our sea-coast, being thus left without any armed vessel, the Board was immediately called together, and our condition in the exigencies of these times considered, and the Secretary of the Navy urgently requested to at once place an efficient war-steamer or armed vessel to cruise off our port and coast for the protection of our commerce. The Secretary of the Navy at once complied with the request and also despatched a Revenue Cutter to do this duty at this port temporarily, until the fine new steam-cutter Mahoning, a powerful and swift steamer, in command of Capt. Webster, was ready for service and was subsequently sent to this station, and rendered most valuable service in these waters for several years thereafter.

The Board subsequently adopted the following: *Resolved*, That we recommend all ship owners to place on board their vessels such armament and additional crew as will protect them against the attacks of the small piratical cruisers which infest the seas, and we recommend our insurance companies to encourage such arming of merchant vessels, by discriminating rates of insurance.

These recommendations were generally adopted by our steamers and larger class vessels.

PRIZE VESSELS.

The Board expressed the opinion, that a proportion of prize vessels, captured from time to time during the war, if brought to Portland could be sold as favorable to interested parties, as at any other port, and with less delay and expense attending the ajudication and sale here, than in any other considerable port on the Atlantic, and the Board adopted a resolution requesting the Secretary of the Navy to thus dispose of vessels sold under reprisal.

A DRY DOCK.

At the annual meeting of 1864 a vigorous movement was made towards building a dry dock at this port, of a capacity sufficient to take out the largest classed vessels afloat. Since the days of building larger class vessels, had rendered our railways inadequate to meet the necessities of commerce, much of which, it had for a long time been evident was being diverted from the port, by the reluctance of shipmasters, in all parts of the world to take freights, or to charter for ports without suitable facilities for possible needed repairs. To this end a committee was appointed to solicit subscriptions to stock, and in five days the necesary amount of $150,000 was subscribed. A charter was obtained and the present dock at Cape Elizabeth was built the following year.

HOTEL ACCOMMODATIONS.

For several years prior to 1864 it was apparent that the want of better hotel accommodation was effecting to turn many traders and business men from the markets of Portland to Boston and other cities, and the Board appointed a committee to confer with capitalists, and to take such measures as would secure ample and first-class public houses. Since which

GEORGE W. WOODMAN.

the hotel accommodation of Portland has been equal to any city in New England.

BUOYS AND STEAM WHISTLES.

Shortly after the wreck of the British steamship, Bohemian, the Board deemed a thorough examination of all the rocks and shoals lying in the vicinity of the approaches of the harbor expedient, for the purpose of ascertaining if all dangers were properly marked by suitable buoys. After such examination the Government was memorialized to cause such dangers to be appropriately marked, which was done by the coast survey. The Board also petitioned for steam whistles at certain dangerous points of approach to our harbors.

PILOTAGE.

Tho Board of Trade being empowered in its charter to appoint a suitable number of pilots for the port of Portland and there never having been any authorized pilots appointed by the Board, the subject was brought before them early in 1864. A committee was appointed to consider and arrange for a voluntary system of pilotage. The committee reported favorable to the appointment of three competent pilots, but fearing such measure might be initiatory to a compulsory system in the future, the subject was indefinately postponed. Meantime, the President and Secretary of the Board of Trade are authorized to issue certificates to competent pilots, when such documents are required, and these Board of Trade certificates are recognized by the London Board of Trade.

BREAKWATER HARBOR LIGHT.

In January 1854 the Board memorialized Congress for a harbor light on the breakwater, and also to rebuild the Custom House (Exchange building) that was destroyed by fire about that time, both of which were subsequently granted, and in April of the same year the Board petitioned the City Council, to request the Superintendent of the U. S. coast survey to make accurate survey of Portland harbor and connecting waters, to establish water lines for wharves, and to increase the depth of water, which was also granted, and elaborate details published of the work.

HARBOR FORTIFICATIONS.

Early in 1857 the Board petitioned Congress for a fortification on Hog Island ledge, and the proper fortification of such other points commanding the entrance of the harbor as might be deemed expedient. Fort Gorges was constructed as soon as possible and was regarded as a formidable fortress at the time of completion, but the Rebellion demonstrated, that long range and powerful rifled ordnance required more extended "out posts," and territory has been secured for batteries to command the more distant approaches to the harbor, which was advised by the officers of the Board.

THE RECIPROCITY TREATY.

The proposed abrogation of the Canadian Reciprocity Treaty, in 1864, engrossed much attention of the Board and a committee, of which Hon. T. C. Hersey was chairman, was appointed to thoroughly investigate the subject in all its bearings regarding the fisheries, the trade, and commerce, not only of our city and State, but of the country at large. The investigations of the committee were thoroughly discussed in open meeting by most of the membership of the Board, who were so unanimously committed to an equitable treaty, that the committee was instructed to attend the commercial convention held at Detroit, Mich., in July 1865, to oppose the abrogation of the treaty which was done in an able speech by President Hersey. And again in Feb. 1866 the Board adopted a series of resolutions to Congress favoring an equitable treaty with British North America, and has several times since, as often as the subject has come before commissioners of either Government, re-affirmed the policy of reciprocal trade to which it was so early committed.

IMPROVED MAIL FACILITIES.

During the Rebellion, when so many people were called from their homes, and the United States Mail increased ten-fold, and the Postmaster of Portland persisted in handling the mails without any increase of force, or improved methods, to the inconvenience and discomfiture of the larger part of the community, many of whom were obliged to wait for hours for postage or the delivery of letters, while the *single* delivery window remained closed for an indefinite time. The Board sent a memorial, together with a unanimously signed petition (14 foot long) of the citizens, to the Post Master General, asking the desired improvements in our postal arrangements, which request was promptly granted, and the Post Master here directed to keep the cashier's window open for the sale of stamps during *all* business hours, also to place boxes at several convenient points, romote from the office, for the reception of letters.

WRECKED EMIGRANTS.

The wreck of the British steamship "Bohemian" off this port on the 22d of February, 1864, by which several emigrant passengers lost all their effects, and were left in a destitute and helpless condition, in a foreign country, among strangers, objects of pity, requiring immediate relief from the charitable, the Board of Trade was believed to be the most direct and effective agency of reaching the public sympathy in behalf of the sufferers, and a subscription was started and some $1.500 and much clothing was contributed, and judiciously distributed to the distressed people, who were all comfortably clothed, fed and furnished with sufficient money to take them to their destination, which act was officially recognized by the British Government.

RELIEF FOR THE SOUTH.

Immediately following the charities in behalf of the wrecked emigrants, $7,671.64 was raised in the same way, through the agency of the Board for the relief of sufferers of the Rebellion in East Tennessee, which was duly acknowledged as follows: "*Resolved*, That on behalf of the people of East Tennessee, we hereby tender our heartfelt thanks to the citizens of Portland for their noble and disinterested zeal in behalf of our suffering people, and to each individual of the tens of thousands in the North who have so generously contributed to save our people from starvation."

A NEW CUSTOM HOUSE.

In the year 1865, the United States Treasury Department submitted to the Board plans for a new Custom House at this port, on the site of the old Custom House, on the corner of Fore and Pearl streets. On examining it, the opinion prevailed that the location was too far east, considering the drift towards the western section of the city, as well as inadequate to meet the requirements of a suitable building for the growing commerce of the port. The Board recommended a location on Commercial street in the vicinity of the entrance of Center street. The government architect approved the plans of the Board, but an appropriation for the purchase of the site failed to pass Congress and the new edifice was erected upon the old location, a mistake obvious to all.

Manufacturing Interests.

The manufacturing interests of the city have always received the generous co-operation of the Board and the influence of the organization has been thrown in favor of all new enterprises of merit. In 1865 the Board appointed a committee to visit some of the leading manufacturers in various other cities of New England and to report such branches of manufactures as could be profitably established in this city, and among other things the committee recommended to the Board the establishment of a joint stock company with a capital of $50,000, for the manufacture of the Johnson's Steam Fire Engines, resulting in their manufacture here. At this time, the buildings of the Rolling Mills were up and the machinery going in. This was also one of the off-spring of the Board. About this time, in 1865, the Board was pushing, with great energy, for a sugar refinery in this city, to stimulate the importations of sugar, and extended aid through committees and otherwise to the Portland Company, the Glass Works, the Shovel Manufactory, Sugar House and various foundries and machine shops, the Kerosene Oil Works, Provision Packing Houses and to boot, shoe and clothing manufactures, as had their origin in this Board, or received its fostering care. In 1873, the Board established a standing committee, under the name of "The Board of Manufactures," and appointed Walter Wells Esq., the eminent statistician, as Secretary, who prepared and issued to the world a prospectus of the advantages and facilities of this city and State for manufacturing. This same committee is still co-operating under the directions of its chairman, Hon. W. W. Thomas, Jr., by conference or otherwise, with all seeking such interests in our vicinity.

TENEMENT HOUSES.

In 1866, the attention of the Board was called by Mr. Beckett, then engaged in taking census of the city, to the great lack of houses for small rents which was operating seriously against an increase of population. The Board took such action as lead to the provision of sufficient accommodation for at least five thousand people in the next twelve months, by pushing into the suburbs, and building pleasant homes.

DETROIT COMMERCIAL CONVENTION.

In 1865 a call was made for a convention of the Boards of Trade and Chambers of Commerce of the United States and British North American Provinces, at Detroit, Mich., on July 11th, for the consideration of the the subjects of commerce, finance, transit, reciprocial trade between the United States and the British Provinces, and other matters, looking to the prosperity of the country and of aiding the general government in the solution of the finances of the country. This Board appointed the following delegates who attended: T. C. Hersey, A. K. Shurtleff, T. E. Twitchell, M. N. Rich, J. S. Bedlow, R. M. Richardson.

Forty-five Boards of Trade and Chambers of Commerce were represented from various parts of the United States and British Provinces, comprising more than four hundred members, many of whom were the ablest men in the country. It was on this occasion that T. C. Hersey, Esq., president of this Board, made his memorable speech in favor of reciprocity in opposition to the Hon. Vice-President of the United States, Hannibal Hamlin, who represented the lumber interest on this occasion. It was also at this convention that the National Board of Trade had its origin.

THE PAYMENT OF TROOPS.

At the close of the Great Rebellion the transportation home and the payment of the soldiers became a question of considerable importance. The plan then existing was that all troops should return to each State Capitol for discharge and payment, and the additional useless expense of transporting all troops from Portland to Augusta, sixty miles distant, and back again through this city was an needless expenditure of at least $30,000, to which this Board of Trade called the early attention of the general government by sending Mr. Lynch to Washington, who laid the matter before the quartermaster general, who ordered a paymaster to be stationed at Portland to pay all troops ordered there.

City Census.

At a meeting of the Board in October, 1865, it was voted to recommend the city to cause the census of the city to be taken at once, and the secretary was instructed to prepare a memorial to the mayor, aldermen and city council to that effect and place the same in the Merchants Exchange for signatures, which having been subsequently presented to the city government was granted, and the census taken, the result of which is elsewhere alluded to.

Great Fire of 1866.

The great conflagration of the memorial year of 1866, when fifteen hundred buildings were destroyed, sweeping eight miles of public thoroughfare, devastating an area of three hundred and twenty acres in the business portion of the city, throwing ten thousand people houseless and homeless upon public charity, and twelve million's worth of property was wiped out, including all the leading business offices and commercial organizations—this money value, however, does not represent the loss of valuble records and documents of history by many societies and corporations. The loss to the Board of Trade by this fire, besides all the property in the Merchants Exchange Room, which amounted to more than $2,000, all the records of the Board, the public documents, charts, maps, official papers, all the large and valuable library, including twenty volumes of Willis's new history of Portland, and many valuable works and reports, records of arbitration, etc., that never can be replaced. In fact nothing was saved from the Board of Trade room but the carpet and some half dozen chairs. All the original records of the Board, which were in the safe, were destroyed. The Exchange

opened, temporary rooms in Mr. D. T. Chase's store, on Long Wharf, and staid there until the next summer, then moved into the new building, corner Exchange and Fore street, and finally returned to its present location early in 1868.

TAXATION OF BANK STOCK.

A repeal of the law taxing bank stock held by non-residents was urged by a majority of the members, prompted by a belief that the present law had the injurious effect of turning capital from our State, as many holders of bank stock were disposing of their shares and withdrawing much capital from our State in this way, which could but exert an injurious effect upon the progress of trade and commerce. A memorial was sent to the legislature praying for a repeal of the law, but finally failed to pass.

NATIONAL EXHIBITIONS.

The Board has frequently taken action to have our city and State creditably represented at the international exhibitions at Paris, London and Frankfort-on-the-Main, also at Berlin, which have resulted in giving some of our packing houses national reputation abroad for the superiority of their productions.

DOCKS FOR IRON-CLADS.

Through the efforts of the Board, a congressional commission was secured to visit this port and examine the facilities, here offered, for constructing docks for the iron-clad naval vessels of the United States. A committee from the Board received the commission and transported them to the mouth of the Presumpscot River. The commission, consisting of Gen. B. S. Alexander, chief engineer J. W. King, of New York, and Melancthon Smith, of Washington, were favorably impressed with our spacious harbor and its fortifications. But League Island was finally chosen for the locality.

REGULATION OF CURRENCY.

Soon after the close of the War, it became evident to the Board that a curtailment of the currency would tend to relieve the commercial embarassment of the country. Resolutions were accordingly adopted and sent to Congress, urging action to this end.

Subsequently the following communication was received from the Secretary of the Treasury:

TREASURY DEPARTMENT,
WASHINGTON, February 16, 1867.

DEAR SIR:

I have the honor to acknowledge the receipt of certain resolutions adopted by the Board of Trade, of the city of Portland, on the 29th ult.

I am pleased to learn that there is one Board of Trade in the United States that takes a sensible view of the currency question.

With thanks for your courtesy in sending me the resolutions, and to the Board for expressing so emphatically correct views upon a very important subject, I am very truly yours,

H. McCULLOCH, Secretary.

To M. N. RICH, Esq.,
Secretary of Board of Trade, Portland, Me.

INSOLVENCY LAW.

Through the efforts of this Board, aided by the late Hon. Chas. McLaughlin, the present State insolvency law was perfected and adopted, and has been regarded by such general favor that the Board has been frequently consulted by the general government in behalf of the preparation of a national bankrupt law.

PORTLAND AND WORCESTER RETURN COMPLIMENTS.

In the fall of 1874 members of the Board of Trade were invited to join the city government with many prominent citizens to make a visit to Worcester, Mass., calling at Nashua, N. H., where the party were joined by a large delegation, which accompanied the Portland delegation, all as guests of the Portland and Rochester Railroad, just completed, to Worcester. The city government of Worcester received and entertained the guests with the most cordial hospitality. Carriages were in readiness and the party taken over the city to view its attractive business advantages, and in the evening an elegant banquet was given at the hotel, at which the most hearty good cheer prevailed, and many warm friendships were formed.

The next year Portland returned the compliment and invited the city government of Worcester and the Board of Trade, also kindred corporations of Nashua, N. H., and several representatives of the press, to be the guests of the city and of the Board of Trade, which was accepted. The party arrived here at noon, passed around the Marginal Way to the Grand Trunk station, where a salute of torpedoes greeted them, and through Commercial street to Railroad wharf, where they embarked on board the steamer for the Islands. Superintendent Tucker had gaily decorated the Eastern Railroad station with flags, and a salute was fired as the train passed through. The steamer went direct to the Islands. The visitors, during the sail down, were busily getting a view at the harbor, the facilities for business, and the scenery, and were loud in their praises. Many prominent citizens of Portland joined on board the steamer, swelling the party to about 350.

At the island, disembarked, and headed by Chandler's Band, marched to the bake, ready to uncover. The tables were set, the company was hungry. Hon. Geo. W. Woodman, president of the Board, called their attention and addressed them briefly, inviting the party to partake at once of the feast. They promptly seated themselves at the table and business commenced. The bill of fare consisted chiefly of 28 bushels of clams, 60 dozen of eggs, 60 dozen ears of corn, 375 lobsters, 1 barrel of oysters, and 1 barrel of sweet potatoes.

In the evening, the city government gave a ball and a supper at the City Hall, which was a most delightful final to this well devised excursion, of which we should have more, as nothing can do so much toward promoting fraternal business relations between communities. The visitors were delighted with their reception, and all expressed a wish to come again. May the friendly relations thus established between the two cities be continued to the end of time.

ELEVATOR AND STORAGE CAPACITY.

There is at present, on Galt's Wharf, in the immediate vicinity of the ocean steamer docks, a grain elevator, built by the Grand Trunk Railroad Co., in 1875, 101 feet in length, 53 feet wide, and 107 feet high, with 42 bins for holding grain 46 feet deep, of a total capacity of 150,000 bushels, all fitted with modern dock elevators and large steam shovels for unloading and loading cars and vessels.

The Board has recently taken action for securing the construction of an additional elevator of not less than 500,000 bushels capacity at this port, and still more will, no doubt be added, from time to time, as fast as the necessities require to meet shipments coming to the port.

There is, at present, ample shed room covering six wharves, for the safe care and protection of merchandise in transit through this port, and with the proposed more ample grain elevators, no other port on this continent will possess more ample and commodious facilities for careful, expeditious and cheap handling of freight, and the custom regulations here are such as to facilitate the passage of merchandise to its destination, with the least possible delay.

Social Meetings.

Towards the close of his life, the Hon. John B. Brown frequently expressed the opinion that it would be an excellent thing for the Board to introduce occasional social entertainments at its meetings, so as to encourage better attendance and to enhance a broader interest with its members, by bringing them together around the "festive board," where more free and unrestrained expression of ideas could be drawn out to the common advantage of all.

The ideas of Mr. Brown were well received, but in the sharp competition of trade, it seemed difficult to fix upon a time to convenience a sufficient number to ensure success to this comparative inovation upon the strickly business character of Board of Trade meetings, but shortly after Mr. Blabon's inaguration at the head of the Board, the subject of a banquet was introduced, and the President expressed his warm sympathy in the project and appointed a committee to arrange for a suitable dinner, at one of the hotels, and arrangements were shortly after perfected for such an entertainment to be given jointly by the Board of Trade and the Merchants Exchange, at the Falmouth Hotel, March 20th, 1886.

One hundred and seventeen sat down to the banquet, after having previously enjoyed social games of cards, or a pleasant chat in the parlors. The crowning success of 'this occasion seemed to be the almost entire absence of speech making—the assurance felt that no one should be called upon to speak removed all restraint, and it was then and there voted to make these dinners annual. Accordingly, on the 26th of March, of the present year, the second annual dinner occured, and was reported in the city *Press* as follows:

"The dinner given by the Portland Board of Trade and Merchants Exchange, one year ago, met with such success that a large attendance was assured for the second annual dinner, the gentlemen who were present on the former occasion being eager to enjoy the festivities of Saturday evening, which had been selected as the time for the dinner of 1887. At the Falmouth, Mr. Martin had made ample preparations for his guests, and they found in the parlors on the front of the house, tables for card playing, while the ladies' parlor was opened for the first time, after being newly decorated and furnished. The members of the Board began to assemble in the hotel shortly after 4 o'clock, and from that time until 7.15 o'clock, when dinner was served, the gentlemen were constantly arriving. The card tables were surrounded, while animated conversation was carried on in the parlors and the broad corridors.

In the large dining room there were 160 covers laid, at three tables extending nearly the whole length of the room and a table across the end of the apartment. Nearly every seat at the tables was occupied, the company numbering about 140. The tables were adorned with fruits and flowers and elaborate designs, the whole with the glittering glass and crockery having an extremely pleasing effect. The dinner was excellently cooked and faultlessly served.

The following is the *menue*:—

                    Blue Points on Shell.
                 Bisque de Homard a la Stanley.
Celery.   Radishes.
                   Baked Trout—Sauce de Vin.
Pommes de Terres Parisiennes.   Asperge—Sauce a la Creme.
                  Turkey—Cranberry Sauce.
Puree Pommes de Terre.   Haricots Verts.
                   Spring Lamb—Mint Sauce.
                          Petits Pois.
              Filet de Bœuf, Pique, aux Truffes.
              Cotelette de Poulette a la Nivernaise.
                 Riz de Veau aux Petits Pois.
                  Oyster Patties a la Creme.
               Banana Fritters—Sauce Venetienne.
                      Champagne Punch.
                     Grouse—Giblet Gravy.
                Mallard Duck—Gelee de Corinthe.
Pommes de Terre Saratoga.   Lettuce a la Mayonnaise.
       Salade de Poulette.   Salade de Homard.
              English Plum Pudding—Sauce Sampion.
Assorted Cake.   Tutti Frutti Cream.   Fruit.
                         Cafe Noir.

President Blabon being absent from the city, Captain J. S. Winslow, vice president of the Board, presided at the head of the table. On his immediate right and left sat Mayor Chapman, Hon. W. W. Thomas, Jr., and the officers of the organization. It was a dinner of eleven courses and it was fully two hours before the cigars were passed around. Captain Winslow, as soon as the dinner was over, announced that there would be no formal speeches, but he had no doubt that any one who wished to speak would be listened to with pleasure. Calls for the mayor and other prominent gentlemen were immediately heard through the clouds of smoke. Mayor Chapman said that it was one of the conditions on which he was present, that he should not be called upon for a speech. Mr. Thomas replied to his called simply by expressing his thanks. Ex-Mayor Walker stated that he could not speak for he should then be guilty of obtaining goods under false pretences. He had promised many, whom he had invited to attend, that there would be no speech making.

The company then adjourned to the parlors, all much pleased with the success of the occasion."

SAMUEL J. ANDERSON.

70

THE MERCHANTS' EXCHANGE.

Directly after the organization of the new management of the Board of Trade in 1863, Mr. M. N. Rich, who was then conducting the commercial news room in the Fox block, on Middle street, suggested to Mr. Hersey and Mr. Jewett the advantages that might be derived to the business people of Portland by uniting his news room with a more eligible one on the lower floor, and arrange for receiving telegraph despatches of the movements of the army and of the flucuations of the market, etc., all to be under the auspices of the Board of Trade. The proposition was received with favor.

The first meeting, to make preliminary arrangements for the present organization, was held at the residence of the late Hon. Jedediah Jewett, and on the 20th of March, 1863, a subscription book was opened. On the 30th of the same month a room was opened in the building formerly occupying the present site, and for many years previous known as Patten's auction and commission house, with a comfortable Board of Trade room in the rear.

Mr. Jewett, who was chairman of the committee on the formation and opening of the Exchange, conceived the idea of having no newspapers on file, but that all the news should be placed on a large blackboard occupying a high place against the wall, and that the room should be open to the public for one hour a day from eleven to twelve o'clock, when the audience should be "rung out" by a Chinese gong, or large bell, and the room be thereafter closed for the day. This plan Mr. Jewett thought would be the most effectual for insuring a prompt and full attendance of business men every day, thereby facilitating the sale and exchange of all kinds of commodities, for which sample tables had been prepared. But the irregularity of the despatches concerning military movements, and the fluctuation of the gold market, soon compelled the abandonment of this programme, and the room was kept open not only all day, but was often crowded on Sunday by eager and anxious throngs during the most critical hours of the rebellion. Mr. Jewett's plan of excluding newspapers was gradually encroached upon, first by admitting a stand for a file of each of the Price-Currents, in the leading cities, and then gradually, other newspapers were suggested by the subscribers.

The new Exchange was very successfully dedicated with a membership of two hundred subscribers, and the increase of its members was so great that it was soon found necessary to remove the Board of Trade room from this to the floor above. The first telegram placed upon the bulletin of the new Exchange read as follows:

"New York, 11.15 a. m. Gold opened at 1.56." On July 11th, 1864, Gold went to 2.85.

Other despatches followed in rapid succession and great enthusiasm was manifested throughout the day. The accessions for the next two weeks carried the membership up to two hundred and seventy, and its increase thereafter was steady and rapid till there were four hundred names on the roll.

In the great fire of 1866, the building was swept away and all the property of the Exchange destroyed, except its records. But in the course of a month, quarters were engaged of the late Mr. D. T. Chase, at No. 2 Long Wharf, and a temporary room furnished in rather a rustic manner. But what these quarters lacked in style and finish, was fully compensated by the extraordinary facilities afforded for fishing.

March 17, 1867, the Exchange was removed from Long Wharf to the second story of the new building on the eastern side of Exchange, corner of Fore street. There was then three hundred and forty members. This room afforded very neat and comfortable quarters for the Exchange, and the Board of Trade was accommodated in the adjoining room. Jan. 22, 1867, the Exchange completed the circuit by returning to the rooms now occupied with three hundred and nineteen members.

It might be interesting to revert to some of the liberal subscriptions of money made in these rooms during the war. Those for the relief of East Tennessee, for the camp hospitals, for the sanitary commission, on account of the great fire at Wiscasset, for the "Bohemian Sufferers," and for the relief of

Savannah, aggregated more than thirty thousand dollars in cash, within five years, for charitable purposes alone.

An act to incorporate the Merchants' Exchange was passed in 1867, with a view of purchasing the land and erecting an Exchange building on the then vacant lot at the corner of Exchrnge and Milk streets, for which $20,000 was actually subscribed, but the general depression of business, which immediately set in at that time, checked any further efforts by the committee.

SUMMARY OF WORK.

The principal work accomplished, and that has from time to time engaged the efforts of the Board of Trade to accomplish and facilitate, since its organization, may be briefly summerized as follows :

Meeting on 'change, May 9, 1853, from 12.30 until 1 o'clock p. m., in front of the post office, memorialized Congress for a harbor light on the breakwater—granted in January, 1854.

1854. Asked for a United States survey of the harbor and establishment of water line for wharves and deepening of water —granted.

1854. Petitioned the United States to remove the custom house and post office—granted.

1856. Prepared suitable dockage and wharfage to accommodate the "Great Eastern," and though she never came the piers are still a proud monument to the enterprise of our city.

1857. Petitioned Congress to open negotiations for an international code to suppress privateering—granted.

1857. Petitioned Congress for a fort on Hog Island ledge to be called "Fort Gorges"—granted.

The International Steamship company had its origin in, and the fostering influences of the Board.

The opening of direct steam communication with New York and Philadelphia was the work of the Board.

The Bangor and Machias steamboat company originated from the regular line of sailing packets established by the Board early in 1864.

The establishment of the Merchants Exchange in 1864 with 355 subscribers—though so shamefully neglected of late years—is a credit to the Board.

In March, 1863, the Boston Board of Trade attempted to divert the trade of the West with Portland by tapping the Grand Trunk at Prescott with a branch to the St. Lawrence, thence by steamers to Ogdensburg, &c., so as to avoid Portland. This Board requested Manager Brydges of the Grand Trunk to meet the Board, which he did and promised that such arrangement should not be made. At the same time, a discriminating rate of freight then existing in favor of Boston, was abolished.

In August, 1863, the Boards of Trade of Detroit, Chicago and Milwaukee visited the city by invitation of this Board. Their entertainment cost over $3,000, but the investment has paid millions in the business it has since opened up. This is enough in itself to justify the support of the Board of Trade if it had never accomplished another thing; but the story is not yet half told.

A standard flour inspection was established in 1864, and it was no fault of the Board that it was not perpetuated after the great fire of 1866.

The steam cutter Mahoning was sent to this port through the efforts of this Board during the war.

In 1863 the want of a dry dock was discussed in the Board, which appointed a committee to obtain subscriptions to the stock, which was all taken in one week and the dry dock built the following season.

Better mail facilities and increased postal advantages of the city were brought about through the efforts of this Board during the war and since.

Wood's marble hotel was erected through the efforts of this Board, and after its destruction, through its further efforts, Mr. Brown, its first president, promised the Board he would build a house that should be an honor to the city as his last public building. The Falmouth is the proud monument of his public spirit.

The supply of water from Sebago lake was vigorously advocated in the Board in 1863, and persistent efforts were made thereafter till the object was accomplished.

Buoys and steam whistles for Cape Elizabeth, Matinicus Rock and Quoddy Head were asked for by the Board, and now give notice of the dangers lying about the approaches to these points in thick weather.

A compulsory pilotage tax upon the commerce of this port was killed by the Board of Trade in 1863.

The proposed tariff on molasses in 1864 was so excessive as to promise serious injury to the business of Portland, and a special committee from this Board went to Washington and succeeded in getting a modified rate of duties.

The Board raised $7,641.16 in 1864 for the relief of suffering Union people of East Tennessee, and $1,500 to relieve the distresses of the emigrants landed here from the wrecked steamer "Bohemian." Nearly $30,000 were raised for kindred purposes through the instrumentality of this Board during the years of the Rebellion.

The Portland Company, Rolling Mills, Glass Works, Shovel Manufactory, Sugar Refineries, and other manufacturing industries have in turn received support and encouragement, and were about all originated by the Board, and if they were not all successful it was from no fault of this organization.

In June, 1865, a committee was chosen to bring about the manufacture of shoes in this city by a joint stock company with a capital of not less than $50,000, which resulted in several firms and individuals entering into the business which has been so successful here.

The Portland & Ogdensburg Railroad was originated by the Board early in 1867, and the first meeting in its behalf was called by the secretary of the Board.

The National Board of Trade was organized chiefly through the efforts of the Portland delegation to the great commercial convention at Detroit in 1867.

The detention of merchandise at Island Pond for entry and payment of duties there for goods coming over the Grand Trunk to Portland, was corrected by the efforts of the Board in 1868.

Negotiations for reciprocal trade with the Canadas have been persistently urged from time to time.

The relief of commerce and navigation by remission of taxation on shipbuilding materials, etc., has frequently been advocated in Congress through this Board.

A Board of Manufactures was established in 1871 by this Board, to encourage and promote in every possible way the investment of capital from abroad in manufacturing interests in this city. An industrial fair in 1875 was one result.

Deepening the harbor by removing the middle ground to admit the largest steamships to the wharves at any time, was the result of the appropriation asked of Congress by this Board in 1872.

Breaking the ice in the upper harbor and around the wharves in extreme cold seasons has been done and paid for by the Board.

The rebuilding of the grain elevator after the fire of 1874 received the earnest co-operation of a special committee from this Board.

The protection of the city from the storage of oils, spirits and other combustible and inflammable materials, in hazardous localities, and the providing of fire boats for the water front and wharf property, have been frequently urged by the Board.

That the city should be always creditably represented in all of the great commercial centres of the world, has been the special care of the Board, where and whenever its influence could be brought to bear.

A department of trade and commerce in the national cabinet, now so generally urged throughout the country, was suggested in this Board in 1878.

The adulteration of food and drugs has been condemned by a strong protest by this Board, and prohibited by law.

The Board has protested against any and all injurious discrimination in rates of freight or monopolies, and has interested itself for the regulation of inter-state commerce.

It has aided in securing mileage tickets for our commercial travellers at the lowest possible rates.

For an equitable distribution of the Geneva award, the Board took early and effective action.

The meeting of the American Association for the advancement of science and of the National Board of Trade in this city, were suggested by the Board.

The perfection of the United States signal service at this port, and the greater efficiency of life saving stations, are due largely to efforts of this Board.

The change of system and removal of some of the light houses on this coast, pressed with an indecent obstinacy, bordering on a spirit of revenge by the light house board, because the people dared to remonstrate against such a dangerous measure—engaged the unceasing efforts of the Board, until the people's will prevailed.

1884. Took action towards co-operating with members of Congress, in devising measures looking to some check on the decline of American shipping, through the so called Dingley Bill, also to aid in perfecting the efficiency of the Revenue Marine Bill.

Co-operated with the state commissioner in making a creditable show of Maine products and works of art, at the New Orleans Exposition.

1885. Secured legislation to suppress evils growing out of itinerant traders and peddlers evading license and taxation by skipping from town to town.

1886. Took action to secure further improvements to the harbor and deeper water, suitable for passages of largest ships at all times of tide, also aided New York Produce Exchange in preparing a revised bill of Lading, to be adopted by all business houses in this country and in Europe—international.

Appointed a commission to co-operate with the Grand Trunk Railway Company, to secure adequate elevator facilities for handling grain at this port.

The fisheries and the troubles on the Canadian borders have been carefully considered, and such action taken in the premises as seemed expedient, while yet the whole matter was in the hands of the Executive, and under treaty.

1887. Petitioned Congress and urged our congressmen to take action to place all our seaports in a proper state of defence, also adopted measures to prevent the diversion of our Railroads from their intended usefulness to our city.

As an arbirator and a mediator in difficulties arising or existing between indiviuals, corporations or governments, tending to hinder the prosperity of the people, have always been promptly and effectively met by the Board of Trade.

All of its good works cannot be written as much is done by constant correspondence, in the way of furnishing statistical information of the business of the port, to other Boards and to commercial houses in all parts of the country, as well as a vast amount of information to Congress and the several departments of the general Government. Yet enough has been mentioned we hope to give an idea to those who sometimes ask "What good is the Board of Trade to Portland?"

JURISDICTION OF THE BOARD
OVER PILOTS AND PORT WARDENS.

The Board of Trade by its charter is alone authorized to appoint pilots and port wardens for the port of Portland, and to issue certificates to such officers under its official seal, and this authority is not only recognized by the Board of Trade of London and by the government of Great Britain, but also by all the principal ports of the world, and though it has not been considered necessary from the well known ease and safety of access of this harbor to regularly appoint and commission pilots, as there always so many experienced pilots at hand, yet the Board has been sometimes called upon to endorse and commission one or more competent persons for special service, as in the case of the visit of the Monarch and other great war ships of the British navy, when the remains of George Peabody were sent over to this country.

As the services of port wardens are almost constantly in requisition to examine the stowage of sea going vessels and ocean steamers, in order to determine condition of cargoes and to certify to damages for adjustment of insurance indemnities. Such officers are regularly appointed, qualified and furnished with an official seal to affix to their official certificate, which are all matters of the most careful record and under the inspection of the officers of the Board. Great care is taken to select only men of large nautical experience, well informed in the methods of commerce and navigation, barratry and all the laws, rules and regulations effecting charter parties and marine insurance, as well as the customs regulations. And when at any time a port warden is found to be incompetent, the Board has authority to vacate the office and fill it with a competent person. The services of the port wardens are paid by fees based upon the character and extent of the services performed. A special office is maintained by the port wardens in close proximity to the shipping, accessible at all business hours.

GEORGE P. WESCOTT.

The nomination of a suitable and competent inspector of grain loading vessels, has also been generally conceeded to the Board of Trade for such officers at this port, which is now performed with ability and satisfaction, by the intelligent reporter for the American Shipping Lloyds at this port. Great care is exercised by the inspector, to protect underwriters—we might here add, also, that the Port Wardens are enjoined by the Board, to exercise great care in certifying to the stowage of cargos, as well as in the handling, so that merchandise suffer as little as possible in the transportation or warehouse.

RULES AND REGULATIONS.

Applications for membership received at any meeting of the Board, or of the managers, lie over until the next meeting of the full Board, before ballot is taken.

ADMISSION FEE to the Board, $3.00.

ANNUAL ASSESSMENTS, payable on the first of January, $3.00.

To the Merchants Exchange, individual, $6.00.

To the Merchants Exchange, firms and corporations, $10.00.

Annual meeting of the Merchants Exchange, March 30th, in each year, when annual assessments commence.

Annual meeting of the Board of Trade, the second Monday of January in each year.

Special meetings of the Board may be called by a majority of the managers, or upon written request of ten or more members.

Stated meetings of the managers, the first Thursday in each month.

A quorum of the Board consists of not less than eleven and of the managers not less than five members, including a presiding officer.

CONSTITUTION.

Article 1.—*Officers.* The officers of this Board of Trade shall consist of a President, three Vice-Presidents, seven Directors, a Secretary, and Treasurer, who shall constitute its Board of Managers; they shall be chosen annually by ballot, and shall hold their offices until others are duly elected and qualified in their stead.

Article 2.—*Annual and Special Meetings.* This association shall hold an annual meeting on the second Monday of January, at half past seven o'clock, P. M., but special meetings may be called by order of a majority of the Managers, whenever they may deem it proper; and upon the written application of not less than ten members, the Mamagers shall call said meeting at the time so requested.

Art. 3.—*Monthly Meetings of Managers.* The Managers shall meet statedly on the first Thursday of every month, for the transaction of such business as may come before them; and at the annual meeting shall present to the association a report of the proceedings of the past year.

Art. 4.—*Committee of Arbitration.* There shall be appointed annually by the Managers, a Committee of Arbitration, to consist of five members; two of whom may be rejected by the parties submitting the case, and their places supplied if the said parties so request, by two other members to be appointed by the Managers.

The Chairman of said Committee shall be designated by the Managers at the time of its appointment.

Art. 5.—*Duties of Committee of Arbitration.* The duties of the Committee of Arbitration shall be to arbitrate and decide all disputed accounts and contracts, and all controversies of a mercantile character, which may be brought before them by the members; the parties having previously signed a bond, for such an amount as said Committee may require, to abide by the decision of the same. The Secretary of the Board shall serve as the clerk of the Committee of Arbitration. Any member who does not abide by, and comply with the decision of the Committee shall be expelled from this Association by order of the Managers.

ART. 6.—*Committee on Railroads and Steamboats.* There shall also be appointed by the Managers, annually, a standing Committee on Railroads and Steamboats, to consist of five members, to whom shall be referred all matters relating to the transportation of merchandise and passengers to or from the city. They shall annually, and whenever they deem it expedient, make reports to the Managers or Board on such subjects relating to the various railroad and steamboat lines connected with our city, with such recommendations for the action of the Managers or Board, as they may deem it advisable.

ART. 7.—*Duties of Secretary.* The Secretary shall keep a list of the members of the Association, and also an accurate record of the transactions of the Managers at their monthly meetings, and of the annual meetings of the members; attend the sittings of the Committee of Arbitration; record their decisions; give notice to said Committee when their services are required; render a copy of their verdicts to the parties in the case; collect the fees of arbitration, and all other moneys due the Board, and pay the same over to the Treasurer; read the minutes of the last meeting at the monthly meetings of the Directors, and annual meetings of the members; and report the proceedings of the Committee of Arbitration, at each meeting of the Managers; and for his services, when faithfully performed, shall receive such compensation as the Managers shall annually fix.

ART. 8.—*Duties of Treasurer.* The Treasurer shall receive from the Secretary all moneys belonging to the Board, shall disburse the same when approved of by the President or one of the Vice-Presidents, and shall report the receipts and expenditures at each monthly meeting of the Managers, and annual meetings of the Association.

ART. 9.—*Funds and Assessments.* The funds of the Association shall always be subject to the control of the Managers, and they shall be deposited in one of the savings banks in Portland, or invested when the amount thereof shall exceed two hundred dollars.

ART. 10.—*Admission of Members.* Any individual (a resident of Portland) may become a member of this Association, on payment of a sum not exceeding ten dollars in advance. Annual assessments may be made, and any refusal to pay such assessment for one year, shall be considered as a withdrawal from the association, and the name of the party shall be stricken from same.

[See Record March 2, 1876.]

ARTICLE 11.—*By-laws—how made.* The Managers shall have power to make such By-laws as they may deem necessary, which shall be binding upon the association unless rejected or amended at the next meeting of the association, to which they shall be submitted for that purpose.

ARTICLE 12.—*Amendments to Constitution.* This Constitution shall not be altered or amended, except at a special meeting called for that purpose by order of a majority of the Managers, a printed notice of which meeting and the proposed alterations shall be transmitted by the Secretary to each member of the association.

BY-LAWS.

ARTICLE 1.—*A Quorum.* The President, or one of the Vice Presidents, shall preside at all meetings of the Board, and also of the Managers. A quorum of the Board shall consist of not less than eleven members, and a quorum of the Managers of not less than four directors, together with the presiding officer; but in the absence of the President and all the Vice-Presidents, a President pro tem. may be chosen.

ART. 2.—*Special Meetings.* The President, or in his absence either of the Vice-Presidents, shall have power on any emergency to call a special meeting of the Board, but the business to be acted upon at such special meeting shall be given in the notice of said meeting, and no other acted upon but by unanimous consent.

ART. 3.—*Admission of Members.* Every person desirous of becoming a member of this association shall be proposed at a stated meeting, and if three or more negative votes shall appear against any candidate, he shall not be admitted a member, nor be again proposed, until after the expiration of six months from the time of said rejection. On becoming a member he shall sign the Constitution and By-Laws.

ART. 4.—*Committee of Arbitration.* The Committee of Arbitration shall render their awards in writing to the parties in controversy, through the Secretary of the Board, within one week after their decision shall have been made.

ART. 5. The fees of the Committee of Arbitration shall be left discretionary with the committee, subject, however, in case of objection, to the approval of the Managers.

ART. 6. Any member desiring the services of the Committee of Arbitration, shall notify the Secretary in writing, and state the character of the case to be investigated.

ART. 7. No member of the association who is cognizant of any fact or facts in a case before the Committee of Arbitration, shall refuse to give testimony before said committee, if notified in writing by the Secretary of the time and place, when and where his evidence may be required; upon pain of expulsion from the association, unless he can give a satisfactory excuse for such refusal.

ART. 8.—*Regular Meetings.* The monthly meetings of the Managers shall be held on the first Thursday of every month, at the chambers of the Board, at such hour as may be ordered by the President; written notice of which meeting shall be given to each member of the Board.

ART. 9.—*Expulsion of Members.* Any member who shall refuse or neglect to comply with the Constitution and By-Laws of the association, may be expelled by the vote of three-fourths of the members present; but a notice of said motion shall be served on him by the Secretary, previous to the day of said meeting.

ART. 10.—*Withdrawal of Membership.* Any member who may wish to withdraw from the association, shall give written notice thereof, but shall not be permitted to withdraw unless he shall have paid his yearly subscription.

ART. 11.—*Fees and Assessments.* In addition to the admission fee, an annual assessment, to be fixed by the Managers, shall be collected by the Secretary, not exceeding three dollars.

ART. 12.—*Honorary Membership.* The Board of Directors, may at their discretion, admit to honorary membership any member of the Board, who in the opinion of its members, may be entitled to some distinguished mark of their respect and gratitude, on account of extraordinary services to the Board, or long and faithful membership, *provided*, that he shall have been proposed at a preceding meeting, and receive a unanimous vote. Honorary members shall not be subject to annual assessments.

ART. 13.—*Port Wardens.* No person shall be eligible to the office of Port Warden who is in any way engaged as Ship Broker, Shipping Master, or any one interested in the importation or exportation of merchandise, or inconsistent with the provisions of Revised Statue Laws of Maine.

PORT WARDENS.

PUBLIC LAWS OF MAINE.

SECTION 23, PAGE 343.   REVISED STATUES OF 1883.

SEC. 23.—Port Wardens, shall be elected in any town or city situated on navigable waters. upon the petition of ten or more citizens engaged in commercial pursuits therein.

SEC. 24.—If in such city or town, there is a Board of Trade duly incorporated, said Board shall annually elect the Port Wardens; otherwise the municipal officers thereof shall annually elect them.

SEC. 25.—Said Boards of Trade by their managers or said municipal officers, shall forthwith on complaint of any person aggrieved, after hearing, remove for cause any Port Warden by them elected, and all vacancies shall be filled by said authorities.

SEC. 26.—Port Wardens shall be men of commercial or nautical experience, and shall hold office one year from each election and until others are qualified in their stead, except when removed from cause, or when elected to serve out an unexpired term; and they shall be sworn to faithfully perform their duties.

SEC. 27.—They shall make a record of their doings and keep the same in their office for inspection at any time free of charge, by any person interested therein.

SEC. 28.—When requested by any person interested, Port Wardens shall proceed on board of any vessel on her arrival in port and survey her hatches, and notice if they are properly caulked and secured; and if they have been opened by some person not a Port·Warden, that fact shall also be noticed, and all the facts in relation to the hatches of said vessel shall be entered in the official record.

They shall also examine the condition and stowage of the cargo of any vessel, and if any portion of it be found to be damaged, they shall inquire into and ascertain the cause thereof, and make a memorandum of the same, noting particularly the marks and numbers of each damaged package, and shall enter the same in full in the records of their office; and for the purpose of ascertaining the extent of said damage, they shall examine goods, wares, or merchandise of any description, in any warehouse or store, or on any wharf, or at any place where the same are, *provided*, that said goods, wares, or merchandise are part of the cargo, and are claimed to be damaged; and they shall note particularly the marks and numbers of every package examined by them, and the extent of the damage received, and all the facts in relation thereto shall be entered in the records of their office.

Sec. 29.—When requested in writing by any person interested, Port Wardens shall also survey the cargo of any vessel arriving in port in distress; and shall make and record in the book of their office, a full and particular report of the condition of said cargo, and of the recommendations in relation to the disposal of such portions of the same, as in their judgment, may not be in condition for re-shipment, reference being had to the best interests of all concerned.

Sec. 30.—When requested in writing by any person interested, they shall also survey any vessel, which may have suffered wreck or damage, or which may be deemed unseaworthy; and such Port Wardens shall call to their assistance one merchant and one shipwright, both of whom shall be competent and disinterested persons, and shall be sworn faithfully to perform their duties in the examination and survey, and said Surveyors and Port Wardens shall examine the hull, spars, sails, rigging and all appurtenances of said vessel, and make and record in the books of the Port Warden's office a full and particular report of all the surveys by them held on said vessel, specifying what damage she has sustained, and what repairs, in their opinion, are necessary to render her again seaworthy; and the aforesaid report shall be presumtive evidence of the necessity of such repairs and of the sufficiency of the same when made.

Sec. 31.—Port Wardens shall be allowed fees to be paid by the person requesting their services, as follows: For survey of hatches, two dollars; for each survey of cargo on shipboard, one dollar; for certificate of stowage of cargo, two dollars; for each subsequent certificate, one dollar; for each survey to ascertain extent of damage, two dollars; for each certificate thereof, two dollars; for each survey required by section twenty-nine, four dollars; for each certificate thereof, two dollars; on each survey as required by section thirty, for each person, two dollars; for each certificate thereof, two dollars.

Sec. 32.—In the cities and towns for which they are elected, Port Wardens shall have exclusive jurisdiction in all matters pertaining to their duties, as specefied in this chapter; and any other person who performs or attempts to perform any such duties. in any city or town, wherein there is a Port Warden, forfeits for each offense one hundred dollars, to be recovered in an action by any prosecutor.

Note.—Port Wardens should have their certificate renewed annually and certified by the Secretary of the Board of Trade, the same to bear the official seal of said Board.

OFFICERS OF THE BOARD OF TRADE

FOR 1887.

PRESIDENT, JOSEPH E. BLABON.

VICE PRESIDENTS,

JACOB S. WINSLOW,   WM. G. DAVIS,   EBEN COREY,

DIRECTORS,

GEO. W. WOODMAN,   SAM'L J. ANDERSON,   GEO. WALKER,
WOODBURY S. DANA,   THEO. C. WOODBURY,   CHAS. J. WALKER,
THOMAS SHAW.

TREASURER, CHARLES S. FOBES.

SECRETARY, MARSHALL N. RICH.

PORT WARDENS,

BENJ. W. JONES,   JAMES L. HOWE.

STANDING COMMITTEES.

Committee of Arbitration.—FRANCIS K. SWAN, RUSSELL LEWIS, HENRY M. HOWES, DAN'L W. TRUE, JOSEPH E. BLABON.

Committee on Railroads and Steamboats.—SAM'L J. ANDERSON, JOHN B. COYLE, FRED'K SMITH, WESTON F. MILLIKEN, PAYSON TUCKER.

Committee on Merchants Exchange.—M. N. RICH, WILLIAM W. THOMAS, WM. ALLEN, JR., THEO. C. WOODBURY, CHARLES S. FOBES.

Meteorological Committee.—CYRUS H. FARLEY, WILLIAM SENTER, M. N. RICH.

Board of Manufactures.—WM. W. THOMAS, JR., WOODBURY S. DANA, H. J. LIBBY, CHARLES E. JOSE, CHARLES S. FOBES, WILLIAM R. WOOD, ALBION LITTLE.

JOSEPH E. BLABON.

PORTLAND, MAINE. 57

MEMBERS OF THE BOARD OF TRADE,
April 7, 1887.

Adams, John M.
Atwood, Levi W.
Allen, Wm. Jr.
Anderson, Samuel J.
Andrews, Sullivan, C.
Allen, Chas. G.
Allen, William, C.
Anderson, Horace.
Brown, Philip H.
Baxter, James P.
Brown, W. W.
Brown, John M.
Blabon, Joseph E.
Barker, Clark H.
Burnham, Geo. Jr.
Bean, Wm. H. W.
Barrett, F. R.
Bailey, F. W.
Burbank, A. L.
Bickford, C. S.
Brown, Philip G.
Bolster, M. E.
Bancroft, Chas. O.
Barbour, E. Russell.
Butler, Harry.
Boothby, F. E.
Bartlett, M. M.
Bain, James.
Berry, Alfred H.
Bartlett, Chas. F.
Best, John L.
Belknap, Chas. W.
Belknap, Chas. B.
Bean, I. S.
Brown, Chas. D.
Corey, Eben.
Cram, N. O.
Champlin, J. P.
Carter, James E.
Cammett, Stephen.
Chase, Chas. H.
Clark, D. W.
Cleaves, Nathan.
Cram, Geo. O. K.
Coyle, J. B., Jr.
Cobb, John C.

Chapman, Chas. J.
Clifford, Wm. H.
Cousens, L. M.
Chisholm, H. J.
Carney, Fessenden V.
Cushing, Chas. A.
Chase, Daniel.
Conley, Elisha W.
Champlin, Augustus.
Cook, Charles.
Chase, Andrew J.
Dana, W. S.
Davis, Wm. G.
Drummond, J. H.
Davis, Hall L.
Deering John W.
Deering, Henry.
Dewey, H. P.
Dennison, E. B.
Dow, Fred N.
DeWitt, John E.
Dow, Sterling.
Dole, Chas. E.
Dyer, Seth C.
Davis, Geo. E.
Dewey, A G.
Dow, Joseph H.
Emery, Mark P.
Emery, Isaac.
Emery, John A.
Emery, Daniel F.
Fox, Henry.
Fletcher, J. H.
Fuller, A. P.
Foster, Geo. F.
Fobes, Chas. S.
Farley, C. H.
Ford, Chas. W.
Farrington, C. J.
Fickett, J. B.
Foye, Chas. H.
Foye, Geo. C.
Gerrish, Oliver.
Gerrish, J. J.
Goudy, L. A.
Gibson, M. S.

Gardiner, N S.
Goding, Marshall R.
Gilman, Joseph E.
Hunt, Geo. S.
Hall, John H.
Hamlen, J. H.
Hinkley, Rufus H.
Harmon, Chas. C.
Hersey, H. W.
Hersey, Seth B.
Haskell, T. H.
Hay, H. H.
Howes, H. M.
Haskell, S. B.
Howe, James L.
Harris, Benj. F.
Hobbs, John P.
Haskell Benj. F.
Haskell, Chas. O.
Hall, James H.
Hinds, A. S.
Hilton, W. K.
Hill, Hollis B.
Hunt, Geo. A.
Hall, Albert B.
Jose, Chas. E.
Jordan, James C.
Jordan, Fritz H.
Jackson, Geo. E. B.
Jones, T. Frank.
Jones, Benj. W.
Josselyn, T. A.
Jones, H. L.
Jost, Daniel F.
Kensall, D. W.
Kimball, Geo. L.
Keazer, James.
King, Joseph A.
Kent, Edw. W.
Knowlton, Wm. J.
Kendall, A. A.
Libby, H. J.
Loring, Prentiss.
Loring, Geo. B.
Libby, F. W.
Leavitt, William.

Latham, W. W.
Lewis, Russell.
Lappin, J. J.
Little, Albion.
Lord, John N.
Laughlin, Alex. T.
Lamson, J. H.
Libby, George.
Little, X. John.
Little, Frank H.
Laughlin, Thos. S.
Milliken, Charles R.
McLellen, Jacob.
Milliken, Weston F.
Milliken, Wm. Henry.
Merrill, Charles.
Martin, John K.
Marrett, James E.
McLellan, E. S. E.
Moore, Geo. M.
Mosher, Thomas B.
Morton, Wm. A.
Nickerson, Peter S.
Noyes, Edward A.
O'Brion, Lewis.
Osgood, H. S.
Proctor, John C. [Hon.]
Putnam, Wm. L.
Perkins, N. M.
Pullen, Stanley T.
Palmer, J. S.
Proctor, John F.
Pierce, Edw. R.
Pettingill, A. J.
Peters, Geo. C.
Pierce, Arthur W.
Payson, Chas. H.
Pennell, Henry B.
Ryan, Washington.
Rich, Marshall N.

Richardson, H. W.
Richardson, R. M.
Ricker, H. H.
Rogers, Alpheus G.
Rumery, Jerome.
Roberts, W. H., Jr.
Rice, Dexter S.
Redlon, Nathan E.
Robinson, J. W.
Smith, Abial M.
Sweat, T. L.
Shaw, Thomas.
Small, S. R.
Smith, James H.
Short, Leonard O.
Senter, William.
Swan, Francis K.
Simonton, W. H.
Stephenson, A. B.
Strout, A. A.
Smith, F. A.
Stanwood, Geo. M.
Smith, Fred'k.
Stockwell, J. W.
Sargent, Charles.
Sargent, Edw. H.
Short, Joseph H.
Smith, Alonzo W.
Soule, Wm. H.
Staples, Horatio.
Strout, Chas. B.
Schlotterbeck, A. G.
Sawyer, F. A.
Stevens, Samuel A.
Shaw, Geo. C.
Stockbridge, Ira C.
Senter, William, Jr.
Smith, Lewis B.
Sylvester, Geo. W.
Shaw, Thomas P.

Snow, Lucian,
Spring, E. G.
Sargent, Horace M.
Snow, D. W.
Shaw, Horace H.
Trefethen, George.
Twitchell John Q.
Thomas, W. W.
True, Geo. W.
True, Daniel W.
Thomas, W. W., Jr.
Thaxter, S. W.
Thomas, Elias.
Tomlinson, Edw.
Tucker, Payson,
Thomas, John P.
Taylor, Howard.
Thurston, Geo. F.
Woodman, Geo. W.
Whitney, Ammi.
Waterhouse, J. W.
Woodbury, W. H.
Wescott, Geo. P.
Winslow, J. S.
White, John S.
Woodbury, Theo. C.
Walker, George.
Winslow, E. B.
Watkins, Geo. H.
Waldron, Chas. P.
Wilson, Bion,
Waldron, Edward A.
Webster, Wm. C.
Williams, M. L.
Webb, James.
Walker, Chas. J.
Washburn, Francis A.
York, Edward H.
York, John W.

Total Number, 257.

OFFICERS OF MERCHANTS EXCHANGE
FOR 1887.

DIRECTORS,

M. N. RICH, WM. W. THOMAS,
WM. ALLEN, JR., THEO. C. WOODBURY,
CHARLES S. FOBES.

REPORTER, HERMAN M. RICH.

MEMBERS OF THE MERCHANTS EXCHANGE,
MARCH 30, 1887.

Allen, Wm. Jr.
Atkinson, Isaac C.
Brown, J. B. & Sons.
Burgess, Fobes & Co.
Berlin Mills Co.
Bailey, F. O. & Co.
Burnham & Morrill.
Bailey, James & Co.
Bailey, Fred'k W.
Blake, Wm. L.
Brown & Josselyn.
Boston & Maine R.R. Co.
Bailey, H. J. & Co.
Bain, Russell & Co.
Corey, Eben.
Curchill, E. & Co.
Conant, Patrick & Co.
Canal Bank.
Chase, Leavitt & Co.
Curtis, J. B.
Cummings, Augustus.
Clark & Chaplin.
Chadbourn & Kendall.
Casco Bank.
Chase, Andrew J.
Cleaves, N. & H. B.
Chapman, C. C.
Cousens & Tomlinson.

Clement, Edwin.
Cram, N. O.
Cushman, Rufus.
Chandler, S. H.
Coe, A. H.
Crocker, Frank C.
Chisholm, Hugh J.
Cumberland Bone Co.
Dana & Co.
Davis, Baxter & Co.
Deering, Henry.
Deering, Milliken & Co.
Dow, Coffin & Libby.
Doten, S. H. & A. R.
Drummond & Drummond.
Drowne, Joseph.
Davis, Hall L.
Dry Dock Co.
Dyer, Chas. A.
Duncan Bros. & Co.
Emery, Waterhouse & Co.
Emery, Isaac.
Emery & Fox.
Eastern R. R. Co.
Emery, John A. & Bro.
Farrington, Ira. P.
Freeman, Ebenezer.
Forest City Sugar Ref'y.

Fletcher & Co.
First National Bank.
Fuller, A. P.
Fessenden, Francis.
Foss, Frank L.
Farmer, James L.
Ford, Chas. W.
Foss, Deering & Baker.
Foss, V. Richard.
Greenough, Byron & Co.
Gerrish, J. J.
Grand Trunk Railway.
Goudy & Kent.
Gibson M. S.
Hunt, Geo. S. & Co.
Hamlin, J. H. & Son.
Hersey, H. W.
Howes, Hilton & Harris.
Hooper Bros.
Hunt, Geo. A.
Haskell, S. B.
Harding, Richard.
Hodgdon, Geo. L.
Holmes & Payson.
Ingraham, C. P.
International S. S. Co.
Ingraham, Geo. T.
Jose, Chas. E. & Co.

Jordan, W. S. & Co.
Jordan, A. W.
Josselyn, T. A.
Kendall & Whitney.
Kensell & Tabor.
Kerosene Oil Co.
Libby, H. J.
Lewis, R. & Co.
Loring, Short & Harmon.
Little, Thos. J.
Little, A. & Co.
Lappin, J. J.
Loring, Ansel L.
McLellan, Jacob.
McLaughlin, Chas. & Co.
Merchants' Bank.
Milliken, W. & C. R.
Maine Steamship Co.
Marr & Littlefield.
Musgrave, John W.
Maine Savings Bank.
Maine Central R. R. Co.
Meguire & Jones.
Martin, John K.
Moore & Wright.
Motley & Co.
Morse & Pinkham.
Mathias, Solomon.
Nash, O. M. & D. W.
National Traders' Bank.
Norton, Chapman & Co.
Nickerson, Josiah.
Nutter, Kimball & Co.
O'Brion, Lewis.

Perkins, J. W. & Co.
Proctor, John F.
Portland Savings Bank.
Portland Star Match Co.
Portland Gas Co.
Pierce, Lewis.
Payson, H. M. & Co.
Portland Steam Packet Co.
Portland and Ogdensburg R. R. Co.
Portland Water Co.
Portland Company.
Portland & Rochester R. R. Co.
Patrons Co-operative Association.
Pettengill, Andrew J.
Quinn, James.
Rich, M. N.
Randall & McAllister.
Reade, Noah.
Ryan & Kelsey.
Ricker, J. S.
Robertson, A.
Rice, C. M. & Co.
Rollins & Adams.
Rich, Charles.
Rich, Andrew J.
Spring, A. & S. E.
Shaw, Hammond & Carney
Smith, James H.
Swan & Barrett.
Stevens, A. B.
Senter, William.

Smith, F. A. & Co.
Sanborn, N. A.
Shurtleff, Aretas.
Smith, Abial M.
Snow, Lucian.
Strout, A. A.
Sawyer, A. H.
Simonton & Randall.
Snow, David W.
Twitchell, Champlin & Co.
Thomas, Geo. A.
Trefethen, George.
Thomas, W. W.
Thaxter, S. W.
True, Calvin S.
True, S. A. & J. H.
Thomas, Elias.
True, D. W. & Co.
True, Chas. H.
Union Mutual Life Ins. Co.
Underwood Co.
Woodbury & Moulton.
Winslow, J. S. & Co.
Woodbury & Latham.
Waldron, F. A. & Son.
Wood, William R.
Woodman, True & Co.
White, D. & Sons.
Walker, George.
Willard, E. G.
Waterhouse, J. W.
Wescott, Joseph & Son.
Waite, E. F.
Watkins, Geo. H.

Total Number, 183.

PORTLAND.

Portland, on Casco Bay, is the commercial metropolis of Maine, a port of entry and seat of justice of Cumberland County, 105 miles N. E. of Boston, and 292 miles S. E. of Montreal, pleasantly situated on a peninsular, about 3 miles in length from E. to W., and rises at each extremity into considerable elevation, 161 feet on the eastern, and 175½ feet on the western extremity, giving the city a beautiful appearance as approached from the sea. Its breadth averages about a mile, though much wider at its eastern termination, and also at its junction with the main land. Its harbor is one of the best on the Atlantic coast, the anchorage being protected on every side by land, the communication of the ocean easy and direct, and the depth sufficient for the largest ships, and is never closed by ice.

The city is regularly laid out and handsomely built, chiefly of brick. Several of the streets are remarkable for their elegance and length, Congress, the principal thoroughfare, extends from Munjoy's Hill on the East to Bramhall's Hill on the West. It is also noted for its beautiful shade trees, of which there are not less than 3000 scattered throughout the town.

Prominent among its public buildings are the City Hall, Court House, marble Post Office, elegant Custom House, and "Falmouth Hotel," one of the most imposing structures in the city, and unsurpassed in appointments.

It contains several flourishing literary institutions and public libraries, and a large number of churches, including Universalist, Unitarian, Congregationalist, Methodist, Baptist, Catholic, Swedenborgian, &c., and a superior school system.

Portland enjoys excellent facilities both for ocean commerce and inland trade. In addition to its superior harbor advantages, it has railway communication with the seaboard for many hundred miles. The Grand Trunk Railway and the Portland and Ogdensburg connects Portland with Montreal in Canada, thereby forming a direct channel for the rich commerce of the river St. Lawrence and of the great lakes, while steamers between this port and Liverpool are constantly crossing the Atlantic. There are also many other railroads centering here, and connecting with all the great systems of the country.

The manufactures of Portland are peculiar to a commercial city. Ship building has been long and successfully carried on until of late. Sugar of every quality is manufactured, and the manufacture of boots and shoes has grown to be very extensive. The financial institutions consist of six banks. The city is lighted with gas and electric lights, and abundantly supplied with pure water. It is remarkably healthy, never having been visited by any contagious diseases, and has a population of 40,000.

The power of Portland, the source of all its power as yet, its anticipated and risen prosperity and wealth, lies in its port, —innumerable islands covered with verdure and trees, near the city, lend a charm more to the beauty of this harbor—is romantically situated and is the deepest on the whole coast of the Atlantic.

She has a weekly line of steamers to Europe for six months in the year, varying in capacity from 2,500 to 4,000 tons each. Also, a fortnightly line comprising ships of great carrying capacity and strength to Brisrol E.

The Glasgow freight steamers also come to this port in the winter months, and occasional steamships from London, as well as large British sailing freight ships, bringing salt or coal, and taking out grain.

There is also a line to Halifax and Yarmouth, N. S.; a line to St. John, *via* Eastport; a line to New York and Boston, and several coast steamers.

Sixty-five railroad trains leave and enter the city daily, having connection with nearly all the roads in New England, and traversing through 119 towns in Maine, by which the business of a population of 278,437 has a direct centre in Portland, which has now, with her Marginal Railway of nearly five miles around the city, unlimited facilities for moving and transferring freight, as cars can pass on to nearly all the wharves, where ships of the largest capacity can lay afloat in 30 feet of water.

The Elevator capacity is	. .	150,000 bush grain,
Other warehouse capacity is	. .	450,000 " "
Elevator transfer " "	. .	30,000 " daily,

with other merchandise transfer capacity almost unlimited.

There are two dry docks, the largest, 425 feet long by 100 feet wide, and the smaller one, 175 feet long by 80 feet wide.

The Banking capital of Portland is . .	$3,500,000
Deposits in Savings Banks, ...	8,000,000
Products of her manufacturing industries .	9,000,000
Sales of merchandise, per annum, . . .	46,000,000
Valuation of the city, ...	31,821,012

The facilities for building cars, locomotives, and steamers are ample for present demands, and railroad iron and steel rails are manufactured quite extensively.

Portland is a half day's sail nearer to Europe than any other port in the United States, and the ingress and egress to her spacious harbor is so safe and easy as to require no system of pilotage.

MARSHALL N. RICH.

CONTENTS.

	Page.
Preface	3
Official Seal	4
Presidents, (terms)	5
Sketches of Presidents	6
Treasurers of the Board	9
Secretaries of the Board	9
Past Active Members	10
Origin and History of the Board	11
Original Officers and Members	13
The Incorporation	14
Early History of the Board	15
Steamship "Sarah Sands"	16
Steamship "Great Eastern"	18
Visit of Western Merchants	19
The Great Clam Bake	21
Important Work of Board	23
Detroit Commercial Convention	29
Great Fire of 1866	31
Portland & Worcester	32
Social Meetings	34
The Merchants Exchange	37
Summary of Work	40
Jurisdiction of the Board	46
Rules and Regulations	47
The Constitution	48
The By-Laws	51
Port Wardens' Laws	53
Officers and Standing Committees	56
Members of the Board	57
Officers and Members of Merchants Exchange	59
Portland's Advantages	61
Duty of the Hour,	65

Cards of Principal Business Firms and Corporations follow.

PORTLAND SAVINGS BANK,
No. 83 Exchange Street, Portland, Maine.

The following exhibit shows the state of the Bank April 16, 1887:

LIABILITIES.

Deposits	$5,976,209.36
Interest	140,228.66
Reserve Fund	292,000.00
Rents	4,142.42
	$6,412,580.44

RESOURCES.

United States Bonds	$ 500,000.00
Public Securities	1,904,740.00
Loans to Corporations	314,500.00
Loans with Collaterals	1,133,180.51
Loans on Mortgages	751,709.05
Real Estate	245,504.22
Bank Stock	98,020.00
Railroad Bonds	1,412,000.00
Railroad Stock	20,000.00
Expense	4,041.61
Premium	9,875.00
Cash	19,010.05
	$6,412,580.44

OLIVER GERRISH, Pres.   **EDWARD A. NOYES, Treas.**

Maine Savings Bank,
No. 198 Middle Street, Portland, Maine.

The following exhibit shows the standing of the Bank April 16, 1887:

EXHIBIT.

Deposits (Depositors 15,182)	$4,415,521.36
Interest	72,162.77
Reserve Fund and Profits	180,434.17
	$4,668,118.30

INVESTMENTS.

United States Bonds	$ 190,000.00
City, Town and County Bonds	1,979,995.00
Bank Stock	21,250.00
Railroad Bonds	1,729,500.00
Railroad Stock	9,000.00
Mortgages	339,189.42
Loans, with Collaterals	61,395.00
Real Estate	116,693.42
Corporation Bonds	185,000.00
Premium	8,891.10
Expense	3,332.10
Cash	23,871.26
	$4,668,118.30

SAMUEL ROLFE, Pres.   **CHAS. FOBES, Vice-Pres.**   **A. G. ROGERS, Treas.**

TRUSTEES:—Samuel Rolfe, Charles Fobes, Mark P. Emery, Rufus Cushman, Daniel W. True, William G. Davis, Eben Corey and Alpheus G. Rogers.

Portland Trust Company,

FIRST NATIONAL BANK BUILDING,

Receives Deposits and Loans Money. Legal Depository for Administrators, Assignees, Guardians, Trustees and Courts. Authorized Trustee or Agent for Corporations. Accepts and Executes Legal Trusts.

INTEREST ALLOWED ON DEPOSITS.

H. J. LIBBY, PRESIDENT.   H. BUTLER, SECRETARY.

TRUSTEES.

HARRISON J. LIBBY, Portland; WILLIAM G. DAVIS, Portland; MARK P. EMERY, Portland; PHILIP HENRY BROWN, Portland; CHARLES F. LIBBY, Portland; WILLIAM W. BROWN, Portland; FREDERICK N. DOW, Portland; FREDERICK ROBIE, Gorham; SAMUEL A. HOLBROOK, Freeport; R. B. SHEPHERD, Skowhegan; ANDREW P. WISWELL, Ellsworth; HENRY S. OSGOOD, Augusta.

EXECUTIVE COMMITTEE.

HARRISON J. LIBBY,   MARK P. EMERY,
SAMUEL A. HOLBROOK,   WM. G. DAVIS.

Northern Banking Company,

No. 53 Exchange Street, Portland, Maine.

CAPITAL $100,000.00.

A TRUST AND LOAN INSTITUTION.

Transacts a General BANKING BUSINESS. A Financial Agent for Individuals and Corporations. Authorized Depository for Administrators, Executors, Assignees, Guardians, Trustees and Courts.

INTEREST PAID ON DEPOSITS.

The DEBENTURE BONDS Issued by this Company are a Safe and Profitable Investment.

SELDEN CONNOR, PRES.   WESTON F. MILLIKEN, VICE-PRES.
CHARLES L. MARSTON, SECRETARY.

EXECUTIVE COMMITTEE.

THE PRESIDENT, ex-officio.

JOSEPH W. SPAULDING,   WILBUR F. LUNT,
HOLLIS B. HILL,   EDWIN STONE.

✢ THE FIRST NATIONAL BANK, ✢

PORTLAND, MAINE.

INCORPORATED JANUARY 4th, 1864.

CAPITAL STOCK, $1,000,000.   SURPLUS $112,256.09.

HARRISON J. LIBBY, President.   J. E. WENGREN, Cashier.

DIRECTORS.

WM. W. BROWN,   H. J. LIBBY,   MARK P. EMERY,   ALBION LITTLE,
PHILIP H. BROWN,   FREDERICK ROBIE,   WM. G. DAVIS.

CANAL NATIONAL BANK,

NO. 188 MIDDLE STREET.

INCORPORATED 1865.   CAPITAL $600,000.

W. W. THOMAS, President.   GEO. C. PETERS, Cashier.

DIRECTORS:

W. W. THOMAS,   ELIAS THOMAS, Vice-Pres.,   JOHN N. LORD,
BENJ. C. SOMERBY,   F. W. BAILEY,   FRANCIS FESSENDEN,   F. R. BARRETT.

MERCHANTS' NATIONAL BANK,

NO. 34 EXCHANGE STREET.

INCORPORATED MAY 1, 1865.

CAPITAL $300,000.   UNDIVIDED PROFIT $175,000.

JACOB McLELLAN, Pres.   GEORGE S. HUNT, Vice-Pres.
CHARLES PAYSON, Cashier.

DIRECTORS.

JACOB McLELLAN,   GEO. S. HUNT,   CHARLES FOBES,   W. S. DANA
J. P. BAXTER,   WM. R. WOOD,   D. W. KENSELL.

NATIONAL TRADERS' BANK,

38 EXCHANGE STREET.

INCORPORATED JULY 17, 1865.   CAPITAL $300,000.

WM. G. DAVIS, Pres.   R. O. CONANT, Vice-Pres.
EDWARD GOULD, Cashier.

DIRECTORS.

RICHARD O. CONANT,   WILLIAM G. DAVIS,   R. M. RICHARDSON,
CHAS. O. HASKELL,   WM. N. DAVIS.

CASCO NATIONAL BANK,

195 MIDDLE STREET.

INCORPORATED APR. 26, 1865. CAPITAL $800,000. SURPLUS $290,000.

STEPHEN R. SMALL, PRES.   JACOB S WINSLOW, VICE-PRES.
          MARSHALL R. GODING, CASHIER.

DIRECTORS.

STEPHEN R. SMALL, JOSEPH WALKER, GEO. P. WESCOTT, AMMI WHITNEY, JACOB S. WINSLOW, EDWARD H. DAVIES, FRANK A. PITCHER.

✻Cumberland National Bank,✻

54 EXCHANGE STREET.

INCORPORATED AUG. 6, 1865.   CAPITAL $250,000.

H. N. JOSE, PRES.   W. H. MOULTON, VICE-PRES.
          W. H. SOULE, CASHIER.

DIRECTORS.

HORATIO N. JOSE, JOHN C. TUKESBURY, CHAS. P. INGRAHAM, JAMES S. MARRETT, DANIEL W. TRUE, NATHAN CLEAVES, WILLIAM H. MOULTON.

✻SWAN & BARRETT,✻

BANKERS,

186 Middle Street, Canal Bank Block,

PORTLAND, MAINE.

RUFUS H. HINKLEY.   GEO. H. RICHARDSON.   HENRY ST. JOHN SMITH.

PULLEN, CROCKER & CO.,

✻BANKERS AND BROKERS,✻

NO. 33 EXCHANGE ST., PORTLAND.

Members of the N. Y. Stock Exchange. Private Wire to New York and Boston. Investment Securities for Sale. New York Correspondents, Charles Head & Co., New York and Boston.

STANLEY T. PULLEN.   FRANK C. CROCKER.

WOODBURY & MOULTON,

BANKERS,

176 Middle Street, cor. Exchange Street,

Dealers in Bonds and Securities,

Personal and prompt attention given to any inquiries.

State, Municipal, Railroad and Water Bonds, bought and sold.

THEO. C. WOODBURY,   WM. H. MOULTON,   EDW. H. YORK.

J. B. BROWN & SONS,

BANKERS,

218 Middle Street, Portland, Me.

Deposits Received. Collections made in the United States, Canada and Europe. Travelers' Letters of Credit issued, available in all European Cities. Sterling Bills drawn on Great Britian and Ireland, and Sight Drafts, (in the currency of the Countries), on Paris, Berlin, and other European Cities.

CORRESPONDENTS.

LONDON,	MELVILLE EVANS & CO.
DUBLIN,	THE MUNSTER BANK.
LEIPSIC,	KNAUTH, NACHOD & KUHNE.
MONTREAL,	BANK OF MONTREAL.
BOSTON,	SHAWMUT NATIONAL BANK.
BOSTON,	FOOTE & FRENCH.
NEW YORK,	CONTINENTAL NAT'L BANK.
NEW YORK,	FIRST NATIONAL BANK.

BUSINESS CARDS.

ARETAS SHURTLEFF,
Banker and Broker,
BONDS, BANK AND RAILROAD STOCK,
NO. 194 MIDDLE STREET,

Three Doors West Canal Nat'l Bank, PORTLAND.

ESTABLISHED, 1854.

H. M. PAYSON & CO.,
BANKERS
PORTLAND, - - - - MAINE.

CHAS. H. PAYSON,   GEO. F. THURSTON,   GEO. S. PAYSON.

---

*PORTLAND*MARINE*UNDERWRITERS*

No. 19 1-2 Exchange St., Portland, Me.

Are prepared to Issue Policies of Insurance on Hulls, Freights & Cargoes.

MARINE RISKS ONLY.

ADVISORY COMMITTEE.—WM. LEAVITT, *Chairman*, (of Chase, Leavitt & Co.,) SETH C. DYER, (of S. C. Dyer & Co.,) FRITZ H. JORDAN, (of W. S. Jordan & Co.) JOS. P. THOMPSON, (of Geo. S. Hunt & Co.,) HENRY P. DEWEY, (of J. S. Winslow & Co.,) HORACE M. SARGENT, (of Sargent, Lord & Skillin,) GEORGE TREFETHEN, (of Geo. Trefethen & Co.)

ALBERT B. HALL, Attorney.

RYAN & KELSEY,
SHIP BROKERS,
AND DEALERS IN
SHIP STORES AND CHANDLERY, PLYMOUTH CORDAGE.
AGENTS FOR THE
NEW BEDFORD COPPER COMPANY,

BRONZE and YELLOW METAL SHEATHING, *in suits, delivered at any convenient port.*

243 Commercial Street, Portland, Me.

WASHINGTON RYAN, S. B. KELSEY.

1835.   OLDEST! CHEAPEST! BEST!   1887.

The ✥ New ✥ England ✥ Mutual

LIFE INSURANCE COMPANY,

OF BOSTON MASS.

Leads all other Companies in its Maine Business!—Why?
Because it is Old!—Conservative!—Safe! Because it has a more liberal policy contract than any of its competitors. Because of the Million dollars paid to the widows and orphans of its Maine policy holders, not a single claim has been contested! Because during its history of over forty years in Maine, the Company's record has been kept perfectly clean.

This Company issues nothing but ENDOWMENT POLICIES, which are fully protected from forfeiture by the Massachusetts laws.

☞ Before insuring elsewhere call upon; or address,

V. RICHARD FOSS, Gen'l Agent.

176 MIDDLE STREET, PORTLAND, MAINE.

—TELEPHONE, 243.—

C. M. RICE & CO.

DEALERS IN

Card · Boards, · Book, · News · and · Colored

=PAPERS=

OF EVERY DESCRIPTION.

ALSO, WRAPPING PAPER, PAPER BAGS & TWINE,

16 EXCHANGE STREET,

PORTLAND, ME.

C. M. RICE,   A. R. COBB.

BUSINESS CARDS.

ESTABLISHED IN 1841, BY H. H. HAY & CO.

H. H. HAY & SON,

DRUGS, MEDICINES & CHEMICALS,

PAINTS, OILS, VARNISHES, DYE STUFFS, &c.,

JUNCT. FREE AND MIDDLE STS.,

HENRY H. HAY, }
CHARLES H. HAY, }

PORTLAND.

A. S. HINDS,

Druggist and Apothecary,

CORNER PINE AND BRACKETT STREETS,

PORTLAND.

JOHN W. PERKINS & CO.

Wholesale Druggists,

AND DEALERS IN

Paints, Oils and Dye Stuffs,

94 & 96 Commercial St., and 2 & 4 Custom House Whf.

PORTLAND, ME.

JOHN W. PERKINS,
BENJ. A. PERKINS,

J. HENRY CROCKETT,
WILLIAM S. KYLE.

BURGESS, FOBES & CO.

MANUFACTURERS OF

WHITE LEAD,

Fine Colors in Oil and Japan,

PORTLAND LIQUID PAINTS.

IMPORTERS OF

ENGLISH VARNISHES AND DRY COLORS.

DEALERS IN

Paints, Oils and Painter's Supplies,

106 and 108 Commercial St.

PORTLAND.

FACTORY,--55 and 57 Munjoy St., 53 and 55 Becket St.

JOHN CONLEY & SON,

IMPORTERS AND DEALERS IN

Newfoundland, Labrador Cod, Straits, Bank, Shore & Neat's Foot

OILS.

PRATT'S ASTRAL OIL,

Paraffine, Rosin, Machinery, and Illuminating Oils.

33 AND 35 COMMERCIAL STREET,

PORTLAND, ME.

JOHN CONLEY,   E. W. CONLEY.

W. L. BLAKE & CO.,
―――MANUFACTURERS OF―――

Fine Engine, Valve and Cylinder Oils,
AND "PORTLAND LUBRICATING GREASES."
―――MANUFACTURERS' AGENTS FOR―――

RAILROAD, STEAMSHIP AND MILL SUPPLIES.
OFFICE, 109 & 111 COMMERCIAL STREET, FACTORY, REAR 23.
PORTLAND, MAINE.

CUMBERLAND BONE CO.,
―――MANUFACTURERS OF―――

⇒Cumberland Super-Phosphate.⇐

Office, 2 1-2 Union Wharf, Portland, Maine.

WORKS AT BOOTHBAY, MAINE.

JOHN J. LAPPIN & CO.,
―――WHOLESALE DEALERS IN―――

FLOUR, GRAIN AND FEED,

Rye & Graham Flour, Oat and Rye Meal, Pressed Hay and Straw,

12, 14 & 16 *Pearl* and 333 & 335 *Fore Street, Portland, Maine.*

CAPISIC MILL, DEERING.

JOHN J. LAPPIN.   THOS. J. LAPPIN.

E. COREY & CO.,
195 & 197 COMMERCIAL STREET,
IMPORTERS AND DEALERS IN

IRON AND STEEL,

Best Refined and Common Bar Iron, Norway and Swedes Bar Iron, Norway and Swedes Shapes, Hoop, Band and Scroll Iron, Oval, Half Oval and Half Round Iron, Horse Nail Rods, Cast, German Blister Steel, Spring and Calking Steel, Tire and Sleigh Shoe Steel, Axles, Side and Elliptic Springs, Horse Shoes and Horse Nails, Wheels and Bent Rims, Hubs and Spokes, Hickory Shafts, Tire Benders, Rasps and Files, Eagle Carriage Bolts. Fifth Wheels and King Bolts, Malleable Castings, Nuts, Cast and Wrought Washers, Smith's Fellows, Anvils, Vises and Screw Plates, Cable Chains and Borax.

CUMBERLAND COAL, CARRIAGE HARDWARE, BLACKSMITH'S TOOLS, &c.

ESTABLISHED, 1801.

J. & E. R. BARBOUR,
DEALERS IN
RUBBER GOODS OF EVERY DESCRIPTION.
AGENTS FOR JARVIS ENGINEERING COMPANY.
STEAMBOAT AND RAILROAD SUPPLIES.
Cylinder and Lubricating Oils, Engineer Supplies, and Steam Machinery Appliances.

8 and 10 Exchange Street,　　　　　Portland, Me.

J. J. GERRISH & CO.
GENERAL RAILROAD & ENGINE SUPPLIES
MANUFACTURERS OF
RAILROAD SIGNAL LANTERNS.
Tin and Sheet-Iron Work to Order.

NO. 41 COMMERCIAL ST., PORTLAND, ME.

Sewall Safety Car Heating Co.
CONTROLS STEAM FROM ANY SOURCE

Perfectly, with entire Safety and the greatest Economy. A single valve in each car, and heat in each managed independently of any and all others. Has been tested from thirty degrees below to fifty degrees above zero, and in all tests of long trains Enginemen declare draught on their engines to be imperceptible.

This system has given perfect satisfaction throughout the winter in daily regular use on Maine Central Railroad. Is being supplied to many New England Roads. Inquiry or inspection will satisfy the most skeptical that in safety, simplicity, economy and completeness it is unrivaled. Inspection of system on regular trains of Maine Central Railroad is solicited.

Illustrated description, Estimates of equipment, etc., furnished on application to

SEWALL SAFETY CAR HEATING CO., PORTLAND, ME.

QUINN & COMPANY.

MANUFACTURERS OF

Steamboat, Locomotive, Tubular, and Upright Tubular Flue and Cylinder

BOILERS

Ships' Water Tanks and Engineers' Supplies,

49 COMMERCIAL, CORNER FRANKLIN STREET.

PORTLAND, ME.

MEGQUIER & JONES,

(Successors to C. A. Donnell,)

Plain & Ornamental Brass & Iron Works.

SHIP AND HOUSE PLUMBING A SPECIALTY.

Iron Work for Buildings, Columns, Lintels, Girders, Window Guards, Patent Sidewalk Lights and Gratings, Wire Guards and Railings.

31 and 33 Pearl Street, Portland, Me.

C. R. MILLIKEN, Pres't. J. W. LEAVITT, Treas.

PORTLAND * ROLLING * MILL,

MANUFACTURERS OF

EXTRA, STANDARD, FOREST CITY,

REFINED AND COMMON

MERCHANT BAR IRON,

FISH PLATES AND R. R. SPIKES,

PORTLAND, MAINE.

ESTABLISHED IN 1808.

DANA & CO.

IMPORTERS OF SALT

AND WHOLESALE DEALERS IN

Dry and Pickled Fish.

Eastern Distributing Agents for

HIGGIN'S EUREKA SALT.

188, 190 and 192 Commercial Street.

HEAD OF CENTRAL WHARF,

PORTLAND, MAINE.

WOODBURY S. DANA.   SAMUEL F. BEARCE.

JOHN A. EMERY & BROTHER,

Commission Merchants

IMPORTERS OF SALT.

Head of Union Wharf,   -   PORTLAND, ME.

JOHN A. EMERY,   HANNIBAL H. EMERY.

W. S. JORDAN & CO.,

DEALERS IN

Ship Stores & Chandlery,

No. 102 Commercial Street,

OPPOSITE CUSTOM HOUSE,

FRITZ H. JORDAN, }   PORTLAND, ME.
WINTHROP JORDAN.

CHARLES J. WALKER & CO.,

WHOLESALE

Boots, Shoes,

HARNESSES AND LEATHER,

157, 159 and 161 Middle Street,

PORTLAND, ME.

CHARLES J. WALKER,   ALFRED H. BERRY.

A. F. COX & SON,

MANUFACTURERS AND JOBBERS OF

Boots, Shoes and Rubbers,

LEATHER & FINDINGS,

PORTLAND, ME.

HORACE H. SHAW,   EDWIN L. GODING.

Shaw, Goding & Co.

MANUFACTURERS OF

BOOTS & SHOES,

No. 160 Middle Street,

PORTLAND, ME.

☞ The largest manufacturers of HAND-TURNS in the State. Every variety of Machine and hand-sewed goods made, to meet the wants of best retail trade.

BUSINESS CARDS.

ESTABLISHED 1866.   INCORPORATED 1883.

PORTLAND CEMENT PIPE AND STONE CO.,

——MANUFACTURERS OF——

SEWER PIPE AND VARIOUS STONE GOODS,

ART TILES, VASES, ETC.

J. W. STOCKWELL, Treasurer and Manager,

No. 24 PLUM STREET, - PORTLAND, MAINE.

BOSTON OFFICE, NO. 72 WATER STREET.

ESTABLISHED 1855.   INCORPORATED 1882.

CLARK & CHAPLIN ICE CO.,

Successors to D. W. CLARK & CO.,

DEALERS AND SHIPPERS OF

I C E

PORTLAND, MAINE.

Storage Capacity, 200,000 tons. Ice houses, Kennebec River, Pittston, Bowdoinham, Sebago Lake, Cape Elizabeth and Portland.

DIRECTORS: D. W. CLARK, *Pres.*, ASHBEL CHAPLIN, *Treas.*, DAVID DINNIS, J. S. WINSLOW, M. W. CLARK.

✸GOUDY & KENT,✸

PORTLAND,

ARE THE LARGEST MANUFACTURERS OF

Confectionery & Bakers Goods

IN MAINE.

JOHNSON'S

——LADIES AND GENTS——

Restaurant and Dining Hall,

No. 43 **EXCHANGE STREET,**

PORTLAND, ME.

GEORGE C. FRYE,

WHOLESALE AND RETAIL DEALER IN

DRUGS, FINE CHEMICALS,

SPONGES, TOILET ARTICLES, &c.,

NOS. 320 & 322 CONGRESS, CORNER FRANKLIN STREET,

PORTLAND, MAINE.

MAURICE, BAKER & CO.,

——MANUFACTURERS OF——

FLAVORING EXTRACTS

AND BAKER'S GREAT AMERICAN SPECIFIC,

Office and Salesroom, 216 Middle Street, under Falmouth Hotel,

PORTLAND, MAINE.

C. H. FARLEY,

NO. 4 EXCHANGE STREET,

——MANUFACTURER OF——

Ornamental Glass for Churches, Cars, Steamboats, etc.,

BEVELED PLATE AND MIRRORS,

Spectacle Lenses Made to Order.

F. O. BAILEY & CO.,

MANUFACTURERS OF

DESKS & SHOW CASES,

Store and Office Outfits,

Agents for Smith & Co.'s Desks, Hall Safe and Lock Co., Howe's Scale Co., Cressey Coffee Mills, Knight Cheese Safes, Popular Oil Tanks, etc.

PORTLAND, MAINE.

WALTER COREY & CO.,

WHOLESALE AND RETAIL DEALERS IN

FURNITURE,

DRAPERY AND UPHOLSTERY GOODS,

Arcade, No. 28 Free Street, - PORTLAND.

IRA C. STOCKBRIDGE,

124 Exchange Street, Portland,

Sheet Music, Music Books, Musical Instruments & Merchandise,

Racks, Folios, Rolls, Brass Instruments, Harmonicas, Orguinetts,

STRINGS AND TRIMMINGS OF ALL KINDS,

MAINE LECTURE AND MUSICAL AGENCY,

STOCKBRIDGE COURSE.

H. J. BAILEY & CO.,

Successors to MARRETT, BAILEY & CO.,

IMPORTERS AND DEALERS IN

CARPETINGS, PAPER HANGINGS,

WINDOW SHADES AND DRAPERIES,

190 & 192 Middle Street, Portland.

O. M. & D. W. NASH,

——DEALERS IN——

Tin Plates, Sheet Iron, Zinc and Wire, Anthony Wrought Iron Furnaces, Registers and Ventilators, Highland Ranges.

RICHMOND STOVE CO RANGES AND FURNACES.

We are the agents for the NEW HUB RANGE with *Gauze Oven Door*. Meats cooked with this Range retain all their juice, and no basting is required.

O. M. & D. W. NASH, NO. 6 EXCHANGE STREET.

BURNHAM & MORRILL,

—PACKERS OF—

Hermetically Sealed Goods,

PORTLAND, MAINE, U. S.

CANNED
- LOBSTERS,
- MACKEREL,
- CLAMS,
- GREEN SWEET CORN,
- SUCCOTASH,
- BEEF,
- MUTTON,
- POULTRY,
- SOUPS, ETC.

Our Goods are Prepared in our own Factories, located at Portland, Maine, U. S.—Scarboro, Maine, U. S.—Pine Point, Maine, U. S.—Harrison, Maine, U. S.—So. Paris, Maine, U. S.—Denmark, Maine, U. S.—Minot, Maine, U. S.—Norridgewock, Maine, U. S.—Port Clyde, Maine, U. S.—Columbia Falls, Maine, U. S.—Little Kennebeck, Maine, U. S.—Casco, Maine, U. S.—Farmington, Maine, U. S.—Dixfield, Maine, U. S.—Auburn, Maine, U. S.—Isaacs Harbor, N. Scotia.—Sober Island, N. Scotia.—Carriboo, N. Scotia.—Port Hood, N. Scotia.—Mainadiew, N. Scotia.—Cape John, N. Scotia.—Harrigan Cove, N. Scotia.—Crow Harbor, N. Scotia.—Beckerton, N. Scotia.—Point Bettay, N. Scotia.—MacDonald's Cove, N. Scotia.—Malagash, N. Scotia.—Tor Bay, N. Scotia.—Port Felix, N. Scotia.—Cuddles Harbor, N. Scotia.—Judigue, N. Scotia.

Received the Award of Gold Medal, Paris, 1878, Silver Medal, London, 1883, Gold Medal, New Orleans, 1884-5, Centennial Medal, Phila., 1876, American Institute Medal, New York, 1874, New England Silver Medal, 1877, Maine State Silver Medal, 1878, for superior quality of their products.

OFFICE AND PRINCIPAL WAREHOUSES IN PORTLAND, MAINE.

BUSINESS CARDS.

Snow Flake

CHARLES P. MATTOCKS,
PORTLAND, ME.

Packer of Canned Goods,

Under the Famous SNOW FLAKE BRAND, registered in the U. S. Patent office.

WINSLOW PACKING CO.

Portland, Maine.

Packers of Canned Goods,

Including Winslow's Corn, under the GLOBE brand, (registered trade mark,) the oldest Canned Goods brand in existence.

Consolidated Electric Lighting Co. of Maine.

AMERICAN SYSTEM

Arc and Incandesent Lighting & Motor Power.

OFFICES & CENTRAL STATION, 12 TO 20 PLUM STREET.

DIRECTORS,

Franklin J. Rollins,   Edward H. Goff.
William R. Wood.   Silas Gurney,
       Frank A. Sawyer.

OFFICERS,

Franklin J. Rollins, President.   Frank A Sawyer, Treasurer.
Silas Gurney, Vice President.   Clarence Hale, Attorney.
     John T. Sawyer, Superintendent.

Doing Entire Street Lighting, City of Portland, by Electricity.

GEO. S. HUNT & CO.
W. I. Importers and Com. Merchants,

EXPORTERS OF COOPERAGE STOCK;

And Agents for Eagle Sugar Refinery, Manufacturers of Yellow Sugars,

169 and 171 Commercial St., PORTLAND, ME.

GEO. S. HUNT, JOSEPH P. THOMPSON. FRED. E. ALLEN.

Forest City Sugar Refining Co.

MANUFACTURERS OF ALL GRADES OF

Powdered, Granulated and Coffee Sugars,

ALSO, CRYSTAL AND SILVER SYRUPS,

Office, 165 Commercial Street, - - Portland, Maine.

GEO S. HUNT, TREASURER.

ESTABLISHED, 1867.

George O. K. Cram,
SUGAR BROKER.

Office, at Forest City Sugar Refining Co.,

164 Commercial Street, - - Portland, Maine.

J. H. HAMLEN & SON,
※ EXPORTERS. ※

AND DEALERS IN COOPERAGE, LUMBER AND GENERAL MERCHANDISE,

No. 305 Commercial Street,

PORTLAND.

J. H. HAMLEN, J. C. HAMLEN.

WOODMAN, TRUE & CO.,

WHOLESALE DEALERS IN

Dry Goods, Woolens, Fancy Goods,

AND CARPETS,

CORNER OF MIDDLE AND PEARL STREETS, PORTLAND, ME.

GEO. W. WOODMAN,   SETH B. HERSEY,   WM. C. WEBSTER.

A. LITTLE & CO.

JOBBERS OF

Dry and Fancy Goods,

236 and 238 Middle Street,

PORTLAND, ME.

ALBION LITTLE,   LEANDER A. WADE.

W. H. MILLIKEN & CO.

COMMISSION,

—AND—

Wholesale Dry Goods,

Small Wares, Notions and Carpets,

164 and 166 Middle Street,

PORTLAND, - - - - MAINE.

BUSINESS CARDS.

ZENAS THOMPSON, JR.

[Successor to J. M. KIMBALL & CO.,]

MANUFACTURERS OF

FINE CARRIAGES & SLEIGHS,

NEW WAREROOMS AND MANUFACTORY,

32 to 38 Union Street, - - Portland, Me.

C. M. & H. T. PLUMMER,

Boiler Makers, Machinists

AND DEALERS IN

Steam and Water Pipes, Valves, Fittings,

RAILROAD AND MILL SUPPLIES,

Nos. 48 to 52 Union Street, Portland, Maine.

RANDALL & McALLISTER,

Coal Dealers,

PORTLAND, ME.

Anthracite & Bituminous Coal

BY THE CARGO AND AT RETAIL.

Philadelphia & Reading Coals, and Iron Co.'s Coals, for Sale by the Cargo.

Coal loaded on to Cars or Vessels direct from POCKETS, Screened in First class order.

☞ Connections with all Railroads running out of Portland.

Offices, 76 Commercial Street, 70 Exchange Street.

TWITCHELL, CHAMPLIN & CO.,

IMPORTERS

—AND—

WHOLESALE GROCERS,

PORTLAND, ME.

JOHN Q. TWITCHELL.   JAMES P. CHAMPLIN.

LYMAN M. COUSENS.   EDWARD TOMLINSON.

COUSENS & TOMLINSON,

——WHOLESALE DEALERS IN——

STAPLE AND FANCY GOODS,

FLOUR AND PROVISIONS,

TEAS A SPECIALTY.   MOLASSES A SPECIALTY.

311, 313 & 315 Commercial Street, Portland, Me.

ESTABLISHED IN 1859.

W. & C. R. MILLIKEN,

Wholesale Groceries,

FLOUR AND PROVISIONS,

157 to 185 COMMERCIAL STREET,

PORTLAND, MAINE.

J. S. WINSLOW & CO.,

COMMISSION MERCHANTS & SHIP BROKERS,

AGENTS REVERE COPPER CO.,

AND WHOLESALE AND RETAIL DEALERS IN

SHIP STORES AND CHANDLERY,

NOS. 135 & 137 COMMERCIAL STREET, PORTLAND, ME.

J. S. WINSLOW.   H. P. DEWEY.

S. W. THAXTER & CO.,

✻ FLOUR, GRAIN AND FEED, ✻

NOS. 2 & 3 GALT BLOCK, COMMERCIAL STREET,

PORTLAND, MAINE.

S. W. THAXTER.   W. H. THAXTER.

No. 38 Central Street, Boston.

NUTTER, KIMBALL & CO.,

IMPORTERS OF SUGARS AND MOLASSES,

MANUFACTURERS AND DEALERS IN

WEST INDIA COOPERAGE,

AND WHITE BIRCH SPOOL WOOD,

NO. 418 FORE STREET, PORTLAND, MAINE.

E. T. NUTTER.   GEO. L. KIMBALL.

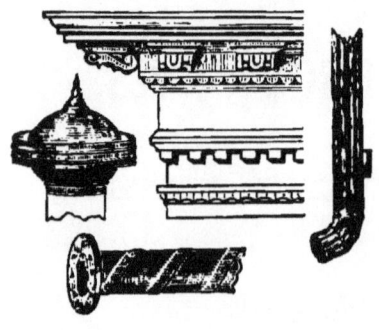

WM. H. SCOTT,

MANUFACTURER OF

Galvanized Iron and Copper Gutters, Cornices, Window Caps, Mouldings, &c.

Agent for Austin's Patent Expanding Water Conductor, Abendroth and Root's Spiral Riveted Pipe, Pumps and Ash Barrels. All kinds of Metal Roofing a Specialty. Also Steamboat, Locomotive Boiler Stacks. Snow removed from roofs. Persons troubled with Leaky Roofs caused by ice and snow freezing on the eaves of the building can have them lined up water tight, or proper ventilation supplied.

WM. H. SCOTT,

29, 31 & 33 Union Street, Portland.

BUSINESS CARDS.

SURETY ON BONDS.

BANK OFFICIALS and others, who are required to give Bonds in their positions of trust, and who desire to avoid asking friends to become their sureties, **or who may** wish to relieve friends from further obligations as bondsmen, should apply to the agents of the

American Surety Company, of New York,

CASH ASSETS, $650,000.   RICHARD A. ELMER, PRESIDENT.

W. D. LITTLE, AGENT,

No. 31 Exchange Street, - PORTLAND, ME.

Refers to Jos. E. Blabon, Esq., President Board of Trade,

TELEPHONE 94.

DOW, COFFIN & LIBBY,
UNDERWRITERS,
—AND—
GENERAL INSURANCE AGENTS,
NO. 42 EXCHANGE STREET.

J. H. COFFIN.   FRANK W. LIBBY.

WM. ALLEN, JR.,
28 EXCHANGE ST., PORTLAND,

FIRE AND MARINE
INSURANCE AGENCY.

Insurance can be placed in this Agency at as Low Rates as at any agency in Portland.

JOHN F. PROCTOR,
—DEALER IN—

Real Estate,

No. 93 EXCHANGE STREET,
PORTLAND, MAINE.

PORTLAND STONE WARE COMPANY,

WINSLOW & CO.,

——MANUFACTURERS OF——

FIRE BRICK,

Shapes and Tiles,

GREASE TRAPS,

CHIMNEY TOPS,

Terra-Cotta Garden Vases, Stone, Ware Beef Barrels,

STONE WARE FOR CHEMICAL PURPOSES,

RED SOLE TILE

——FOR——

UNDER-DRAINING,

And Dealers in

FIRE CLAY,

FIRE MORTAR,

KAOLIN, ETC.

DEPOT AND YARD,

At Eastern Division of the B. & M. Railroad, Charlestown District.

OFFICE,

8 LIBERTY SQUARE,

——AND——

8 BATTERYMARCH STREET,

BOSTON, - MASS.

Factory, North End of Deering's Bridge,

PORTLAND, ME.

J. N. WINSLOW.
P. O. BOX, 1538.

E. B. WINSLOW.
TELEPHONE 549-B.

MARK P. EMERY,

Commission Merchant,

MANUFACTURER AND DEALER IN

COOPERAGE STOCK OF ALL DESCRIPTIONS,

PACKING BOXES OF ALL SIZES, MADE TO ORDER,

324 Commercial Street,

HEAD OF BROWN'S WHARF,   PORTLAND, ME.

BERLIN MILLS COMPANY,

MANUFACTURERS AND WHOLESALE DEALERS IN

SPRUCE LUMBER,

Clapboards, Shingles, Laths and Pickets,

OFFICE, BERLIN MILLS WHARF,

PORTLAND, ME.

ISAAC EMERY,

SHIPPING AND COMMISSION MERCHANT,

AND MANUFACTURER AND DEALER IN

COOPERAGE STOCK,

No. 208 Commercial Street,

PORTLAND, ME.

GILBERT M. SOULE,

MANUFACTURER OF

LONG AND SHORT LUMBER,

Office and Wharf, 418 Commercial Street,

PORTLAND, ME.

MILLS AT GROVETON, N. H.

B. A. ATKINSON & CO.,

House Furnishers,

Corner Pearl and Middle Streets,

PORTLAND,

Have the Largest and Best Selected Stock of

CHAMBER FURNITURE,
PARLOR FURNITURE,
CARPETS AND RUGS,
STOVES AND RANGES,

IN THE COUNTRY.

Examination of Goods and Prices Respectfully Solicited.

ISAAC C. ATKINSON, Manager.

GLEN HOUSE

White Mountains, N. H.

This widely known Favorite Summer Resort, (New 1885), Open June 28th to October 1st, 1887,

C. R. MILLIKEN & CO., Proprietors.

C. R. MILLIKEN,   E. A. GILLETT.

FALMOUTH HOTEL,

PORTLAND, ME.

The Largest and Most Elegantly Appointed Hotel in Maine.

Just refitted and furnished with new and costly Furniture, and every luxury usually found in First Class Hotels.

JOHN K. MARTIN, - - **PROPRIETOR.**

BURBANK, DOUGLASS & CO.

IMPORTERS AND WHOLESALE DEALERS IN

CROCKERY AND GLASS WARE,

Lamp Goods, Chandeliers, and Plated Ware,

NO. 242 MIDDLE ST., PORTLAND.

ALBERT L. BURBANK,   LINCOLN R. LORING.

✻✻✻ WEBB & CUSHING, ✻✻✻

MANUFACTURERS OF

LADIES' AND MISSES'

Fine Boots and Shoes

NOS. 79, 81 AND 83 CROSS STREET,

PORTLAND, ME.

The Mercantile Agency.

Established in New York, 1841; Boston, 1843; Portland, 1868.

EDWARD RUSSELL & CO.,

81 MILK STREET, BOSTON.

Also in Portland and Bangor, Maine, Worcester and Lynn, Mass.

R. G. Dun & Co., 314 and 316 Broadway, 83 Wall Street, and 61 Park Street, N. Y., and in all the leading cities in the United States and Canada, embracing ONE HUNDRED SIXTEEN branch and associate offices.

We have extraordinary facilities, through these numerous connections, of furnishing accurate information respecting the CREDIT AND RESPONSIBILITY OF BUSINESS MEN throughout the country.

OUR REFERENCE BOOK

Issued quarterly, contains the location, names and occupations of over 1,100,000 merchants, traders, manufacturers. bankers and business men generally.

COLLECTION DEPARTMENT. No organization in the entire country offers such secure, prompt and economical means of collecting over due claims as this agency.

Terms of Subscription may be obtained of

EDWARD RUSSELL & CO.,   (T. FRANK JONES, Manager.)

31 B EXCHANGE STREET, PORTLAND.

Portland Business College.

DAVIS BLOCK, OPPOSITE CITY HALL.

This institution offers superior facilities for preparing young men and ladies for the counting room and business pursuits. Terms very reasonable, in fact never so low as at present, while the advantages offered have never been equalled.

The public are cordially invited to call and examine our new rooms and our manner of doing business. Catalogues free. Any further information cheerfully furnished.

L. A. GRAY, Principal, - PORTLAND, ME.

Ayer, Houston & Co.,

——MANUFACTURERS OF——

WOOL HATS, IN ALL COLORS,

BY THE CASE ONLY.

Salesroom, No. 22 West Houston Street, New York.

FACTORY, PORTLAND, ME.

"It Stands at the Head,"

One touch of the finger should produce any character used by the operator of a writing machine; instruments that fail to accomplish this are deficient and do not fully meet the necessity that brought them forth. These facts are self-evident.

The No. 2 "Caligraph" is the only writing machine that fully economizes time and labor, and economy of time and labor is the best reason we know for soliciting trade.

Granting that we are at the front in this, we can show that our late improved machines excel in mechanical merit, durability, and beauty of work.

Over 15,000 "Caligraphs" are in Daily Use.

We publish 400 letters from prominent men and firms which are convincing.

The "Caligraph" is used by the Board of Trade.

For specimens, etc., address,

❋W. M. BELCHER & CO.,❋

NEW ENGLAND AGENTS,

38 Bromfield Street, - BOSTON, MASS.

The Maine Central Railroad,

The Great Railroad Thoroughfare of the State, extends from Portland to and beyond Bangor, to Boundary Line of Maine and New Brunswick, uniting the Railroads of the United States and Maritime Provinces.

This road, with its immediate connections REACH EVERY PART OF THE STATE, the most important Branch,—that from Bangor to Bar Harbor—having been completed in 1884, forming the

ONLY ALL RAIL ROUTE TO MOUNT DESERT.

Time of Express Train between Boston and Bar Harbor, 10 hours. Nor is this famous resort the only one to which this road leads, as it is also the route to be taken for

MOOSEHEAD and the RANGELEY LAKES,

And all the noted Hunting and Fishing Resorts of Maine and New Brunswick, as well as to Boothbay, Camden, Northport and numerous other points along the sea coast and in the interior, which, with their invigorating atmosphere, are drawing increased numbers of visitors each year.

PULLMAN SLEEPING CARS are run on night trains between Boston, Bangor, and Bar Harbor, Bangor and St. John, St. John and Halifax; and Pullman Parlor Cars on day trains between Boston, Bangor and Bar Harbor. The completion of the cantilever bridge across the St. John river at St. John, renders through cars between Boston and Halifax a possibility.

The Portland, Mt. Desert and Machias Steamboat Company,

Is also, Under the Same Management.

Steamers make semi-weekly trips between Portland and Machiasport, leaving Portland Tuesdays and Fridays at 11 p. m., or on arrival of train leaving Boston at 7 p. m., touching at Rockland, Castine, Deer Isle, Sedgewick, Southwest and Bar Harbors, Millbridge, Jonesport and Machiasport, or passengers for the last three named points can take train to Bar Harbor and connect with steamer there.

Persons desiring to get rid of threatened epidemics will find more delightful places in Maine than any other part of the whole country.

Through cars run from Boston, via Boston & Maine R. R., Eastern and Western Divisions, and Tickets and information can be obtained at their depot and city offices, as well as at all Maine Central and principal ticket offices throughout the country. Send for Time Tables.

PAYSON TUCKER, Gen. Manager.
F. E. BOOTHBY, Gen. Pass. Agent.

PORTLAND, MAINE.

Boston & Maine R. R.

THE DIRECT ROUTE
via
BOSTON OR WORCESTER,
—TO—
NEW YORK, THE SOUTH AND WEST.

LOW FARES AND FREQUENT TRAINS
—TO—
ALL THE GREAT BEACHES.

Scarboro, Pine Point, Old Orchard, Saco and Biddeford, Kennebunk, Wells, Salmon Falls, Great Falls, Dover, Rochester, Lake Winnipesaukee, Portsmouth, Exeter, Haverhill, Newburyport, Lawrence, Lowell, Nashua, Clinton, Worcester, Salem, Lynn and

BOSTON.

PARLOR & PULLMAN CARS ON THROUGH TRAINS.
TICKETS TO ALL POINTS WEST AND SOUTH.

JAMES T. FURBER, Gen'l Manager.

DANA J. FLANDERS, Gen. Pass. Agt.

M. L. WILLIAMS, Gen. Agent.

PORTLAND.

PORTLAND & ROCHESTER R. R.

THE POPULAR ROUTE
TO
Manchester, Concord, Nashua, Lowell, Worcester,

SPRINGFIELD,

NEW YORK,

PHILADELPHIA, BALTIMORE,

WASHINGTON,

AND

ALL POINTS SOUTH.

THE SHORT, QUICK ROUTE
TO
BUFFALO, CLEVELAND,

DETROIT, TOLEDO,

CHICAGO, ST. LOUIS,

AND ALL POINTS WEST.

NO TRANSFERS. RAPID TRANSIT. ELEGANT PASSENGER COACHES.

☞ TICKETS AT ALL PRINCIPAL TICKET OFFICES.

BAGGAGE CHECKED THROUGH TO ALL IMPORTANT POINTS.

Depot in Portland, Foot Preble Street.

J. W. PETERS, Superintendent.

Portland & Ogdensburg R. R.

—FOR—

Westbrook, So. Windham, Sebago Lake, Steep Falls, Baldwin, Hiram, Brownfield, Fryeburg, No. Conway, N. H., Bartlett, N. H., with connections for North Windham, Naples, Cornish, Porter, Keazar Falls, Freedom, Denmark, Lovell, Stow, Chatham, via Daily Stages; and Bridgton, No. Bridgton, Harrison, Waterford, via Bridgton & Saco River R. R.

THE FAVORITE PLEASURE ROUTE TO

"Profile," "Crawford," "Fabyan" and "Glen" Houses,

SUMMIT MT. WASHINGTON,

—AND ALL POINTS IN—

WHITE MOUNTAINS.

Bethlehem, N. H., Lancaster, N. H., Whitefield, N. H., Lunenburg, Vt., St. Johnsbury, Vt., Morrisville, Vt., Johnson, Vt., Highgate, Vt., Swanton, Vt., Littleton, N. H., Lisbon, N. H., Bath, N. H., Woodsville, N. H., Wells River, Vt., Montpelier, Vt., Waterbury, Vt., Burlington, Vt., St. Albans, Vt.

——THROUGH TRAINS DAILY TO——

MONTREAL AND OGDENSBURG,

With connections at St. Johnsbury for Newport, Sherbrooke and Quebec. At Burlington for all points on Lake Champlain, Lake George and Saratoga. At Norwood and Ogdensburg for points in Northern and Central New York, Niagara Falls and

THE WEST.

TO SHIPPERS!

The PORTLAND & OGDENSBURG R. R. is the only line now maintaining traffic arrangements with the "FAST FREIGHT COLOR LINES" for direct shipments between Portland and all points West.

✢MAINE STEAMSHIP COMPANY.✢

SEMI-WEEKLY LINE BETWEEN

PORTLAND AND NEW YORK.

One of the staunch steamships, WINTHROP, (new), Capt. Albert Bragg; ELEANORA, Capt John Bennett, leaves Franklin Wharf, Portland, every Wednesday and Saturday at 6.00 p. m. Leaves Pier 38, East River, New York, every Wednesday and Saturday at 4.00 p. m.

Fares, (in State Room), between Portland and New York, $5.00. Round trip tickets, allowing stop over at Martha's Vineyard, $8.00. Between Portland or New York, and Martha's Vineyard, $4.00. Round trip tickets from Portland or New York to Martha's Vineyard and return, $7.00. Meals extra.

Freight received and forwarded to and from all points south and west of New York and east of Portland. For freight or passage apply to

J. B. COYLE, Jr., Gen. Agent, Office, Franklin Wharf, Portland.

HORATIO HALL, Agent, Office, Pier 38 East River, New York.

PORTLAND STEAM PACKET CO.

DAILY LINE OF FIRST CLASS STEAMERS BETWEEN

PORTLAND AND BOSTON.

The STAUNCH AND ELEGANT STEAMERS of this OLD AND RELIABLE LINE leave Franklin Wharf, Portland, every evening (Sundays excepted), at 7 o'clock, arriving at Boston in season for connection with the earliest trains on all diverging lines.

RETURNING, leave India Wharf, Boston every evening, (Sundays excepted), at 7 o'clock in summer and 5 o'clock in winter, connecting on arrival with all railroad and steamboat lines for eastern points. No loss of business time in traveling by this favorite route.

SUNDAY TRIPS DURING SUMMER.

J. B. COYLE, Manager.   J. F. LISCOMB, Gen. Agent.

GENERAL OFFICES, PORTLAND, MAINE.

BUSINESS CARDS. 103

The Passenger Accommodations of the Steamers of this Line are Elegant.

The new and elegant steamers "State of Maine" and "Cumberland," or the favorite steamer "New Brunswick," run regularly the year round between Boston, Portland, Eastport and St. John. The latter named steamer runs from April to November from Boston to Annapolis, Nova Scotia, via Digby. For detailed time table see daily papers.

J. B. COYLE, Manager.   PORTLAND, ME.   E. A. WALDRON, Gen. F'g't & Pass. Agt.

PASSENGER FARES.

Boston and Portland, $1.00.   Boston and Eastport, $4.00.
Boston and St. John, $4.50.   Boston and Calais, $4.50.
Portland and St. John, $4.00.   Portland and Eastport, $3.50.
Portland and Calais, $4.00.

BUSINESS CARDS.

LORING, SHORT & HARMON,

WHOLESALE AND RETAIL

Booksellers and Stationers,

AND DEALERS IN

PAPER HANGINGS,

✢ MANUFACTURERS OF BLANK BOOKS, ✢

LANCASTER BUILDING, OPP. PREBLE HOUSE,

474 Congress St., - PORTLAND, ME.

✺ UNION MUTUAL ✺
Life Insurance Company,

PORTLAND, MAINE.

INCORPORATED 1848.

JOHN E. DeWITT, President.

Assets December 31st, 1886,	$6,124,716.82
Surplus (Mass. and Maine standard),	375,021.98
Paid Policy Holders more than,	22,000,000.00

Send to the Company or any of its Agents for circulars explaining the Maine Non-Forfeiture Law and the attractive plans of the Union Mutual.

www.ingramcontent.com/pod-product-compliance
Lightning Source LLC
Chambersburg PA
CBHW031353160426
43196CB00007B/801